how to attract, house and feed birds

Walter E. Schutz

This Book Belongs to Valerie Norris.

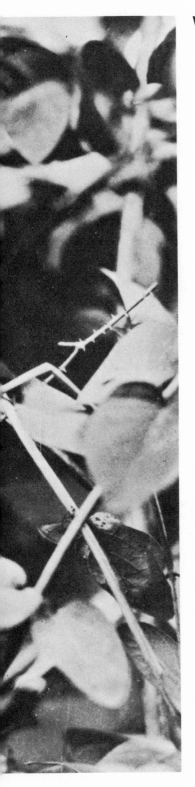

how to
 attract,
house and feed

birds

Formerly published as **Bird Watching, Housing and Feeding**

COLLIER BOOKS
Macmillan Publishing Company
New York

COLLIER MACMILLAN PUBLISHERS
London

We wish to acknowledge and thank the following for giving us permission to use photographs:

page ii	Catbird feeding young	U.S. Department of Agriculture
page x	Canada Goose nest, Oregon	U.S. Department of Interior
page xii	Curlew	U.S. Department of Interior
page 12	Morning Doves	no credit
page 49	Wild Turkey, West Virginia	Courtesy of the American Museum of Natural History
page 50	Catbird #285620	Courtesy of the American Museum of Natural History
page 67	Bluebird by J. J. Audubon	Courtesy of the New York Historical Society, New York City
page 103	Passenger Pigeon by J. J. Audubon	Courtesy of the New York Historical Society, New York City
page 104	Red-Shafted Flicker with Young	U.S. Department of Agriculture
page 114	Egrets, Everglades	Florida State News Bureau
page 183	Blue Jay	Courtesy of the American Museum of Natural History
page 184	Horned Owl	U.S. Department of Agriculture

The first edition of this book was published under the title **How to Build Birdhouses and Feeders.** The second edition, titled **Bird Watching, Housing and Feeding,** was published by the Bruce Publishing Company, Milwaukee.

Macmillan Publishing Company
866 Third Avenue
New York, N.Y. 10022

Library of Congress Catalog Card Number: 74-115299
ISBN 0-02-011910-0

First Collier Books Edition 1974

15   14

Macmillan books are available at special discounts for bulk purchases for sales promotions, premiums, fund-raising, or educational use. For details, contact:

Special Sales Director
Macmillan Publishing Company
866 Third Avenue
New York, N.Y. 10022

Printed in the United States of America

acknowledgments

I wish to take this opportunity to extend my continued thanks to all the people whose valuable guidance has been so helpful to me in the preparation of my books: Owen J. Gromme, John L. Diedrich, and Murl Deusing of the Milwaukee Public Museum; Dixie Larkin of the Wisconsin Audubon Camp; Frank Bellrose of the National History Survey Division at Urbana, Illinois, and the Plankinton Packing Company; Mr. and Mrs. Ralph Morse of the Ned Hollister Bird Club, who supplied information on field trips and bird photography; and Mr. and Mrs. David Cox also of the Ned Hollister Bird Club, who provided information on bird banding.

My thanks again go to Andrew Bihun, Jr. of **The Audubon Magazine,** who offered many helpful suggestions in addition to permission to use material from the magazine, and to Robert J. Woodward, who graciously offered the use of several pictures. Special thanks go to my wife, whose valuable suggestions have resulted in more practical feeder designs and to my son, Tom, who contributed forty-two bird identification illustrations that greatly enhance the book.

Walter E. Schutz

contents

food: the first requirement

water: the second requirement

shelter: the third requirement

some helpful hints

foreword

As in the two previous editions, **How to Build Birdhouses and Feeders** and **Bird Watching, Housing and Feeding,** this completely new and revised edition emphasizes how to attract, feed, and house birds.

Reorganized into six easy-to-find units, **How to Attract, House & Feed Birds** contains updated suggestions on how to lure and keep birds in your area by providing the proper food and housing. Clear, easy-to-follow instructions for constructing well-designed feeders and shelters are provided. These plans are detailed enough for the novice, yet they challenge the experienced craftsman.

As every birder and bird watcher knows, birds are not only beautiful to look at, they provide a vital link in helping to keep the balance of nature. This interrelationship of bird and man, with each other, and with their common environment, is explored in a discussion of ecology in Chapter One. Birds are helpful to man in many ways—meadowlarks and many other birds contribute to plant growth by dropping seeds; sea gulls help keep rivers, harbors, and beaches clean; sparrow hawks and owls catch rodents; and so forth. Yet man's disregard for maintaining conditions that support bird life has resulted in endangering some species of birds.

To help us better understand these wild creatures, bird-migration maps and new tabular material showing how birds are helpful to man are included. For the reader who wants to continue the fascinating study of birds, a valuable reference guide is provided at the end of the book.

Let me close by saying that I hope you, the reader, derive as much illumination, enjoyment, and creative satisfaction from reading this book as I did in writing it.

Walter E. Schutz

ecology today

One of the characteristics of man is his continuing drive to progress. Perhaps his ability to use tools is one reason for this. Through constantly improved tools and technology he has progressed from the cold, inhospitable cave to the push-button home; from smoke signals as a means of communication to satellites; from walking to flying—even to the moon. His accomplishments for his well-being are almost beyond belief.

But everything is not ideal. The industrial colossus, or giant, which man's ingenuity and productivity have developed, and which has brought so many benefits to mankind, has a shadow, too. And the shadow is black—very black in-

1

deed. It covers the fields, the streams, the cities, the forests, the air, even the highest mountains. It is everywhere. No square foot of the earth escapes—no animal, plant, or creature of any type escapes it. The shameful shadow is pollution.

no escape

Almost every newspaper or magazine contains an article on pollution. On radio and TV we are told and shown to what extent this plague is affecting us. The one hope is that steps are now being taken to bring some light into this dismal and threatening area. We will never be able to eliminate the shadow entirely, for we cannot undo the past, but we can influence the future through effective education, regulation, and personal involvement.

The pollution of our streams and rivers is known to all of us. Water, so essential to life, is becoming a carrier of death! Almost every stream, lake and river is polluted, and the outlook for the near future is dark. A recent survey made by the Department of Health, Education and Welfare disclosed that the nation's drinking water systems are unsanitary. About 8,000,000 people in the area checked are drinking water from municipal water systems that contain more bacteria than allowed by Federal standards. Seventy-six out of seventy-nine water systems tested showed that they contained harmful pesticides, too. The pollution of our air is even worse than that of the water. Invisible deadly gases hang like a pall of death over our largest concentrations of population. Although many of the deadly gases are invisible, some of the suspended particles block out the healthful rays of the sun. And since air has no limiting barriers, it can float over endless areas, contaminating the highest mountain peaks and the lowest valleys—there seems to be no escape.

who's to blame?

Most of the accusation is directed toward industry and, rightly so. But, industry alone is not to blame for all of this. Agriculture—common dirt farming—must bear its share of guilt. Rachel Carson's Silent Spring points out how the indiscriminate use of pesticides, if continued, will bring death and famine to our very doors. These harmful products have not only eliminated many of our helpful agents on the face and oceans where they are destroying the water life.

Right along with the damage brought about by agriculture is that caused by lumbering. About one-third of our land is timberland. This resource is still threatened, although for some reason or other conservation efforts have been more successful here than in any other natural field. Many years ago we recognized the need to regulate lumbering and began reforestation programs. Today we are keeping just about even. If we ever cut back our forest conservation programs, we will be faced with a serious lumber shortage, since the use of forest products will increase rapidly and in direct proportion to the increase in population.

what's the answer?

We all know there is no easy answer to all these problems. We know we cannot eliminate the shadow of negligence in one single action. We can take legislative action, and proper legislation at the right point will help us arrive at some of the answers. But there is no one solution to the thousands of problems. Only when the necessity of finding these solutions is given its proper priority can we really begin.

why worry?

One element of our natural resources that is affected and in great danger is our wildlife. We all know of the extinction of the passenger pigeon, and the similar fate of the Merriam elk and the heath hen. In all, about thirty species of wild life have been eliminated in the last 150 years, and about ninety other species are in danger of being lost for all time. These species include fish, animals, and many birds.

To the uninterested, the usual reaction is "So what? What do I care if the otter is no longer here? Why should I bother if the passenger pigeon is no longer in the sky, or the number of robins this spring is fewer than last spring? So what if I don't see as many redheaded woodpeckers as I did before? I've other troubles to worry about!" True, we all have many worries, and having fewer birds may seem a trivial matter. But when you get involved and examine the facts, you find that this is not a trivial matter after all. The number of wild birds in the nation has declined in direct proportion to the amount of deadly pollution we have brought down upon ourselves. And, as the number of birds decreases, the chances for our own survival also decreases. It is as simple as this: The survival of our wild birds bears a direct relationship to our own well-being.

wild birds, one of the answers

It's odd that saving our wild birds is usually regarded as being for the birds' sake alone or because we'd feel bad if there were fewer birds—we'd miss the singing and the brilliant flashes of gay plumage flitting through the trees. Rarely do we hear or read that it is just good sense and good business to save these wild birds. Hardly anyone has ever taken the time or had the initiative to show how we unwittingly depend upon a healthy and numerous bird population in balance with the rest of the natural world. Even Rachel Carson seems to slight this phase of bird conservation.

The companionship of a large number of birds on the feeder is exciting and a great pleasure, but there is much more at stake than this. The value of birds to human beings is beyond general knowledge; it is to everyone's advantage to maintain a healthy and adequate bird population.

twenty box cars of seeds

Here is what is happening every day of the year, yet hardly anyone is aware either of the fact or its importance.

Some years ago a study was made for the state of Iowa by the Department of Agriculture. The study concerned the amount of obnoxious weed seeds consumed by birds for one year. The common sparrow was studied, and it was found that each bird ate about one fourth of an ounce of seed each day.

Little enough you say—granted. But if we estimate that there are only 10 sparrows in each square mile—an exceedingly low figure—and that the season covers only 200 days of the year, we find that these few birds consumed 1,750,000 pounds of seeds! This is about 875 tons or the equivalent to 20 box-cars of seeds. Multiply this by all the seed eating birds, include the seed diet of birds that eat both seeds and insects, and you have a figure that staggers the imagination!

The results of another study made by the Department of Agriculture are shown in the accompanying table. The table shows the findings based on a total of 13,919 birds investigated, plus an unspecified number of additional species. In all cases the percentage of animal or vegetable consumed, as well as the kind of seeds and insects, was established.

Study this table carefully and see the enormous number of harmful insects that were eliminated by the birds. Note too, that of the fifty species of birds covered by this study, sixty percent of the bird's diet is animal, that is, insects or small rodents, and forty percent is vegetable, such as seeds, disease scales, and grasses.

Economic Value of Some of Our Most Common Birds

Source: U. S. Department of Interior Bulletin

Bird Investigated	Animal and Insect	Vegetable
Bluebird	68 Percent	32 Percent
	Beetles Grasshoppers Caterpillars 15 other noxious bugs	Weed seeds such as: Wild blackberry Chokeberry Pokeberry Ragweed Sorrel Virginia creeper Bittersweet Sumac Rose haws, etc.
Robin	42 Percent	58 Percent
	Ground beetles Grasshoppers Caterpillars Angleworms and other bugs	Wild fruits Dogwood Wild cherry Wild grape Greenbrier Holly Elderberry Sumac Many other seeds Crabgrass Cranberries Blueberries
South Carolina Chickadee	83 Percent	17 Percent
	Grape vine insects Black olive scale	Mostly weed seeds

Western Bluebird	82 Percent	18 Percent
	Grasshoppers Beetles Misc. bugs	All noxious weed seeds
Chickadee and Titmouse Family	68 Percent	32 Percent

	Tent caterpillar
	    and eggs
	Flies and bugs
	Beetles
	Plant lice
	Weevils
	Spiders
		Small weed
		    seeds
		Wild fruit pulp
		Poison ivy
		    seeds

House Wren	98 Percent	2 Percent
	All harmful insects Grasshoppers Beetles Caterpillars Bugs and spiders	Bits of grass Few weed seeds
Brown Thrasher	41 Percent	59 Percent

	All harmful insect
	    diet before
	    fruit is ripe
		Raspberries
		Currants
		Wild fruit and
		    seeds
		Some oats and
		    corn

Catbird	44 Percent	56 Percent

	Ants, beetles
	Caterpillars and
	    grasshoppers
	    constitute
	    three-quarters
	    of diet. Balance
	    is bugs,
	    spiders, etc.
		One-third is
		    cultivated
		    fruits
		Strawberry,
		    raspberry
		    and
		    blackberry
		Balance is wild
		    fruit and
		    some seeds

Brewer Blackbird	32 Percent	68 Percent

	Cutworm and
	    pupae
	Cotton boll worm
	Corn ear worm
	Codling moth
		Fruit
		Grains
		Weed Seeds
		20 percent of
		    vegetable
		    diet is of
		    cultivated
		    crops

Towhee	80 Percent	20 Percent
	Hibernating beetles and larvae Potato beetle	Seeds Small wild fruits
Sparrows	33 Percent	67 Percent
	Beetles Weevils Leaf Beetles Grasshoppers Wasps and bugs	Hard seeds Grass and weed seeds Very little oats
House Finch	2 Percent	98 Percent
	Misc. bugs	Weed seeds (62 percent) Wild fruits (27 percent) Grasses (8 percent) Grains (1 percent)
Crow	20 Percent	80 Percent
	Grasshoppers White grubs Caterpillars Weevils Wireworms Small toads and snakes Some birds' eggs	Waste corn and grains in winter Cultivated fruits Wild fruits Misc. seeds
Blue Jay	22 Percent	78 Percent
	Grasshoppers and eggs Caterpillars Click beetles Wire worms Tent caterpillar Brown-tailed moth Weevils A few wild bird eggs One-third of animal diet is of beneficial insects	Wild fruit Acorns Beechnuts Hazelnuts Wild fruits Cultivated corn and fruits
Phoebe	89 Percent	11 Percent
	Noxious insects Click beetles The Phoebe insect diet is exceptionally beneficial.	Small wild fruits No cultivated fruits or grain

Bullock Oriole	79 Percent	21 Percent
	Black olive scale, very large amount Beetles Lady bugs Ants and bees Wasps	Fruits, eight percent of which are cultivated
Meadow Larks	74 Percent	26 Percent
	Beetles Grasshoppers Crickets Cotton boll weevil Grubs	Weed and other hard seeds Waste corn and clover seed in winter Ragweed Smartweed Barnyard grasses
Baltimore Oriole	84 Percent	16 Percent
	Caterpillars Beetles Bugs and ants Grasshoppers Click beetles	Wild fruits Some weed seeds
Red Wing Blackbird	26 Percent	74 Percent
	Beetles Weevils Grasshoppers Dragon flies	Weed seeds Ragweed Grass seed Smartweed No fruits Corn, wheat and some oats make up eight percent of vegetable diet
Woodpeckers	75 Percent	25 Percent
Redheaded Downy Hairy Flicker	Wood boring beetles Wood boring ants Grasshoppers Caterpillars All fruit and fruitwood insects	Small wild fruits and berries Weed Seeds Beechnuts

Swallows	100 Percent	
	All airborne flies and ants Amount eaten is beyond calculation.	
Nighthawk	100 Percent	
	Almost every type and kind of insect June bugs Dung beetles Leaf chafers Wood borers Weevils Bugs, moths, flies Grasshoppers Crickets Mosquitoes Colorado potato bugs Cucumber beetles Bark beetles, etc.	
Cuckoo	90 Percent	10 Percent
	Hairy caterpillars Beetles Grasshoppers Sawflies Stinkbugs Spiders Tent Caterpillars Crickets	Weed and grass seeds No fruits or cultivated grains
Bobwhite	40 Percent	60 Percent
	All destructive agricultural pests such as: Colorado potato beetles Cucumber beetles Bean leaf beetle Squash ladybug Wireworms May beetle Corn billbugs Weevils Army worms Cotton Boll weevil Cutworms	All worst weed seeds: Crab grass Cockspur Witch grass Sheep sorrel Smart weed Bind weed Pigweed Corn cockle Chickweed Ragweed, etc. Wild fruits and berries Small amount of grain

Bobolink	30 Percent	70 Percent
	Misc. bugs and insects	Mostly weed seeds Wild rice No fruits
Kingbird	90 Percent	10 Percent
	Almost entirely of noxious insects and pests which makes the Kingbird very beneficial	Small native fruits No cultivated fruits or grain
Grackles	25 Percent	75 Percent
	All injurious insects No birds' eggs as usually believed	Waste grain in winter and spring Cherries Blackberries 20 percent of vegetable diet is of cultivated crops

smothered in bugs!

True, some cultivated crops are also eaten by the birds and we hear about this from farmers and gardeners and I suppose they have a legitimate complaint. However, what would these same people say if they were smothered by the 875 tons of weed seeds, the millions of harmful insects, and disease scales these birds eliminate for them? Then they would have a complaint that would be serious indeed! The air would be so full of bugs and flying insects we could not breathe. The fields and woods would be denuded of every blade of grass and every leaf, and we would have to wade knee-deep in these crawling bugs, gnats, and insects.

Meanwhile, the land available to all wildlife continues to shrink as our population increases. The construction of homes, roads, shopping centers, and superhighways swallows up tremendous amounts of acreage that was formerly in grass and forests. Marshes and wetlands are being drained at a rapid rate. In addition, toxic sprays are reducing the bird population alarmingly.

more than a hobby

We should think of these things when we lightly dismiss bird watching as just a pleasant hobby. We should think twice and seriously when we hear of birds being imperiled, because it is not only their existence but our own as well that is being threatened.

Viewed from this standpoint, bird watching takes on an entirely new meaning and should be given much more importance. Perhaps we need a more descriptive word for our hobby than "bird watching" because this usually designates only the pleasure we get. Perhaps we might better describe this absorbing activity as "bird husbandry."

There are many ways in which bird watching can help stem the destruction of our bird population. The best place to start is at the local level. National organizations are doing excellent work, but just as much and more can be accomplished in every city, town, and hamlet throughout the nation. To begin with, find out what is happening in your own area. Have you adequate parks? Are areas being set aside as wildlife refuges? Do you have a Boy or Girl Scout troop that is interested in nature studies? Is there a conservation group with which you can work? Does your area have adequate laws to protect wildlife? Are there other people in your vicinity with the same respect for nature that you have? If so, get in touch with them and form a group or club to promote conservation so that your children and grandchildren will have a beautiful and healthful world to grow up in and enjoy. There are many societies that will welcome your support.

bird watching

ornithology and bird watching

Ornithology and bird watching are so similar and yet so different. Both are based upon the same activity—the study of birds. The difference depends upon the direction and intensity of the study.

Ornithology is a serious business, as is any scientific study of animal or plant life. The ornithologist is usually a researcher, a college professor or other scientist who studies the life, habits, ancestry and other facets of bird life from a clinical point of view.

13

The bird watcher also studies the birds, but his goal is entirely different; usually it is one of personal pleasure. Bird watching includes the person who casually throws out a few bread crumbs once in a while and also the one who maintains a regular feeding program, providing a water supply summer and winter, and who makes a record of all the birds that come to his feeder. He knows when the first rose-breasted grosbeak arrived, how many juncos he feeds during the winter, and so forth. He may participate in the Christmas bird count, or he may not even know the difference between a nuthatch and a chickadee. It can be extended to any length—pleasure is gained out of every minute devoted to it. This perhaps is the reason why bird watching is so popular.

Also, the casual bird watcher, through intense study, may become an ornithologist. The bird count may lead to a year-round study of the number and kinds of birds observed. This may lead to bird banding which in turn commences an intensive study of individual species. This information may be sent to the local chapter of the Audubon Society and in a short time the bird watcher has become an authority on some phase of bird study. He may become an ornithologist and submit findings and reports to a central bureau.

Ornithology and bird watching—both are pleasurable experiences and return so much to those who follow these pursuits. So think seriously about these activities. You will discover, as have thousands of others, that you are entering a new pleasurable and profitable pastime. Try it and see.

Bird watching provides many advantages for the hobbyist. The person who becomes interested in it adds much to his store of knowledge and, as a by-product, frequently is led into other related valuable activities. It is very flexible, for you can devote as much time to it as you please and yet enjoy it the year around. You can work alone or you can enjoy it as a group activity. And, finally, you will make a contribution to your community when you pass on to others, especially young people, the information and experiences gained from this fascinating pastime.

In another part of this book I pointed out the difference between Ornithology and Bird Watching—Ornithology is a serious, scientific study of bird behavior, anatomy, and characteristics, and Bird Watching is mainly a fun hobby.

birding and birders

There is another group that has given itself the name of "Birders." They do not like or appreciate the image of the Ornithologist who is the "absent-minded professor" or the Bird Watcher who is thought of as the "dowager in the baggy tweeds clutching a pearl-covered opera glass in her hand and all a-twitter with her darling children of the forest"!

The Birder is neither of these. He is a person who basically likes the outdoors, a person who takes an active interest in nature about him and is a conservationist at heart. He likes the idea of attracting and feeding birds. He tries to identify as many as possible and keeps a yearly record of what he sees and when he sees it. He likes long hikes into the country with his family and friends. He usually belongs to a local Audubon club and turns in his records each year so that they may be added to the national bird-study figures. He is serious about his hobby up to a point. It's a no-nonsense endeavor, yet he derives a great deal of pleasure out of the activity. His hobby serves a very useful purpose since the information he gathers is so vital a part of our overall study of present-day ecology. There are about three million people who are part of this activity, constituting a sizeable proportion of the total population who are Birders.

Birding brings people, old and young, out into the open country, into fresh air away from smog and poisonous gases. It encourages hiking and walking that is so beneficial to everyone, and, above all, it affords complete relaxation of mind and body—a clear mind at peace and ease.

So, if you are engaged in this hobby, set your goal to becomming a Birder instead of being just a Bird Watcher. At any rate, enjoy the hobby the way you want to enjoy it. No matter how much or little you contribute, you know you are following a worthwhile activity that pays handsome dividends. Good luck!

it's simple to get started

There is nothing complicated or expensive in getting a start in bird watching. You need no costly equipment, machinery, tools, or clothing. Nor do you have to spend money

15

for lessons. All you need is the ability to enjoy what nature is offering you. As a matter of fact, bird watching can be as simple as looking out of a window or sitting on a porch. Many people "window-feed" birds on a board attached to an outside windowsill on which they place table scraps or bird feed. Thus bird watching can be an excellent hobby for the shut-in as well as for those who want to pursue it on an indoor-outdoor, winter-summer morning-evening basis.

how to attract birds

There is really nothing difficult about getting birds to come to your yard and feeders. Perhaps the most important requirement is patience. It will take some time to get birds to make regular visits to your premises. I have had birds alight on a new feeder within an hour after it was erected, but this is the exception. Birds are naturally wary of anything new, but after you have gained their confidence, their trust and friendliness will prove surprising. Their needs are simple, and they ask for little. All they want is food, water, and shelter. If you try to duplicate these as they are found in nature, you are bound to attract birds to your yard and garden. Remember, birds do not like "spic-and-span" surroundings. A brush pile, dead limbs, nearby trees, or possibly some weeds will provide them with the cover and perching facilities that their sense of security requires.

As your interest in this new hobby increases, you will want to know more about certain birds which you would like to

You can obtain the confidence of birds. Provide enough food, avoid noise, move slowly, banish all cats, and you will have birds as close companions.

16

Milwaukee Public Museum Photo

attract to your garden. When you become familiar with them you will learn their likes and dislikes. Soon you will become an experienced bird watcher and you can tell others about your interesting experiences.

all kinds of activities

Most people get into bird watching because it is easily begun, absorbing, and conducive to getting out-of-doors. Although there are many advanced fields for specialists, most people find enough challenge and interest in fields already familiar to us.

Specialized bird-watching activities are pursued by ardent devotees throughout the country. These activities are many and varied and, indeed, in some cases, become lifelong avocations. For example, if you care to specialize, you can become an expert in a particular area. Or you might cooperate in organizing an ornithological society with concrete objectives, such as publishing a local or state book on bird watching. You can also specialize in bird photography and perhaps even sell your pictures to magazines. You can become an expert in bird migration or take up bird banding. Another intriguing specialty is the recording of bird songs and calls.

It is not the purpose of this book to explore all these allied activities in detail. However, the beginner should be aware of the possibilities of the hobby, in addition to mastering the essentials of feeding and sheltering birds. There are many other areas of special interest that can be cultivated.

equipment needed

For more serious bird watching, a pair of binoculars will be helpful to bring distant birds up close for identification. You need not purchase the largest and most expensive pair you can find. Remember that on a long hike you do not want to carry excess weight. Tell a reputable dealer what you have in mind and rely on his advice. Be sure that the binoculars are adjusted before you buy them. They should be kept in a carrying case when not in use.

Another important aid to the bird watcher is a field notebook. An inexpensive, 4 x 5-inch loose-leaf book that you can buy in the five-and-ten-cent store will serve the purpose well. The notebook should be light and have a minimum of pages. In this book you can make notes on your observations (see "Bird Lists," p. 23). This information, which

17

Bird watching provides a relaxing and healthful form of recreation whether one is alone or with good friends.

can be filed according to bird groups when you return home, will become valuable reference material.

Some bird watchers make a life-size drawing of the outline of a bird, print several duplicate copies and insert them in their book. When an unfamiliar bird is seen, the markings, size, colors, and other features can be quickly indicated on one of the outline drawings for later study and identification. These printed outlines are a great convenience for both the inexperienced and the experienced bird watcher.

The more advanced bird watcher sometimes finds additional items of equipment necessary. At a later date you may want a telescope that can be mounted on the door of your car or in a window of your home to command a sweeping view of your yard or the area in which you are driving. Telescopes are made in a range of types and prices that will meet a wide variety of needs.

To complement your growing knowledge of birds, you may decide to start a home library. You can select titles from the excellent variety of classic books that have been on the market and keep abreast of new publications by watching advertisements in newspapers and magazines and checking book-review sections. (See page 189)

An excellent counterpart to a collection of bird books is a record library of bird songs and calls. Within the past few years a number of fine albums have become available and it is a thrilling experience to listen to them. You will be pleasantly surprised to find out how repeated playing of these recordings will help to identify birds. Advanced bird watchers sometimes depend on hearing to identify a bird, and in some instances it is a more accurate means of positive identification.

As far as wearing apparel for field trips is concerned the only suggestions are that you dress for the weather and wear something that will help you blend in with your surroundings. Overshoes or waterproof shoes are in order if the ground is wet or, your hike is going to take you into swampy or flooded lands.

the fun of a field trip

After you have enjoyed the birds that come to your yard and garden, you can begin thinking about taking a field trip, the main objective of which is to find, identify, and study birds. To start you can make it a sort of combination picnic-bird-hunt.

As you gain experience, you will plan your hikes in some detail. You will find that they will be most profitable if you can traverse a variety of habitats such as open fields, shores, marshes, and woods. Take along your binoculars and other equipment. When you reach a spot where you want to do concentrated observation, look for natural cover such as a tree or bush to hide behind. You can also use a screen to conceal yourself. I have used a regular deck chair with a supported canvas roof. With the chair placed in a quiet spot on the lot of our summer home, and the roof pulled down as far as possible, I sat perfectly still for 20 minutes or so and found that robins and flickers both came to within 3 or 4 feet of the chair.

Experienced bird watchers make their field trips either alone or with not more than one or two other persons. There may be occasions when you will have to travel in larger groups. If your trip is to be worthwhile, your companions should be bird watchers too. Sudden movements and sounds will drive birds away. If the group consists of members of your local bird club, you can learn a lot from the experienced bird watchers.

Family groups can enjoy a field trip together since bird watching appeals to old and young alike.

Hendricks—from the National Audubon Society

Trips can last a few hours, a whole day, or several days. Some hobbyists devote many of their vacations to this healthful activity.

Trips can also be planned for your local Boy Scout and Girl Scout troops or some other group of young people with whom you are associated. Since larger groups reduce the effectiveness of a field trip, the participants should be advised beforehand to heed signals for quiet.

when to look for birds

Your first few field trips will undoubtedly be made sometime during the day. As you gain more knowledge and skill in bird watching, you will discover that the best time to observe birds is the early morning—the earlier the better. Some bird watchers arise long before dawn and get settled in their favorite watching spot before the sun is up. If you can do this, you will be handsomely rewarded.

If you want to see owls, you will have to get out just at dusk or a little after. With a strong flashlight, you will be able to spot some interesting flights. You probably will be struck by the quiet flight of these birds, which seem to glide through the trees like gray shadows.

nesting habits of some of the common birds and where you are apt to see them[*]

1. Higher branches and treetops: Blackburnian warbler, cerulean warbler, warbling vireo, wood pewee, Baltimore oriole.

2. Tree trunks and hollow branches: Woodpeckers, crested flycatcher, bluebird, sparrow hawk, screech owl, chickadee, tufted titmouse, starling.

3. Saplings and lower branches of trees: Robin, wood thrush, bluejay, red-eyed vireo, scarlet tanager, rose-breasted grosbeak, redstart.

4. Higher bushes and saplings: Yellow- and black-billed cuckoos, yellow warbler, chipping sparrow, mourning dove, goldfinch, cedar waxwing, kingbird.

5. Low bushes: Field sparrow, song sparrow, chestnut-sided warbler, catbird, cardinal, brown thrasher.

6. On the ground: Ovenbird, black and white warbler, junco, veery, towhee, bobwhite quail, whippoorwill.

how and where to find birds

Certain things must be borne in mind if field trips are to be successful. First, bird watching cannot be done along busy streets and highways. It is true that some birds will be found in inhabited areas, especially during migrating seasons. It is best, however, to look for places that are removed from human activities. These may be a wooded fencerow out on a farm, a pasture along a river or stream, a hill, a swamp or marsh, the beach along a lake, or a mill pond. The more secluded the location, the more apt you are to find the birds for which you are looking.

As shown by the sketch on page 22, there are definite areas in which specific birds live. There are treetop birds which are seldom seen along the ground and there are ground birds which should not be sought in treetops. The information presented here, through the courtesy of the Audubon Society, shows where the bird watcher can expect to find certain species of birds. This is where they nest and this is where he is most apt to see them.

Some birds such as the woodpeckers and flickers inhabit woods with heavy tall trees. Meadowlarks and similar spe-

[*]Courtesy The National Audubon Society.

21

cies will be found in open areas. Even a few hundred feet will make a difference in the kind of birds you see. Gradually, you will find a number of favorite observation posts. To attract the birds after you are on location and the birds are settled down, try making a kissing sound on the back of your hand. The noise will cause the birds to become inquisitive and they will come close. Many stores carry a small bird call made with a rosin stick that produces a squeak. These calls are very helpful in attracting birds. In these hideaways you will enjoy watching and listening to the birds and you will find that their chirping and singing is as pleasant as the sight of the birds themselves.

If your city has a museum, you can study some of the mounted birds. A local zoo may have an aviary that will also prove helpful, and in your library you are sure to find a number of books that show and list the birds that might be seen in your area.

how to identify birds

The scope of this book does not allow space for a detailed treatment of bird identification, although some of the techniques used will be mentioned. The serious bird watcher should obtain one of the several excellent books that are available. They include valuable background information, colored pictures that make identifying birds easy, and they are small and light enough to take along on field hikes.

The average person knows the difference between a pigeon and a crow. But only study and practice will enable him to distinguish one type of warbler or vireo from another. Basically, bird identification consists of placing a bird within its group. The hobbyist does this by learning the characteristics of the chief groups of birds. These general traits include the overall size, the general shape, color, special markings on the body, wings, tail, and head, voice, actions (is he sedate and rested or does he jump around a lot?), and flight characteristics. The beginner should learn where birds are found and what type of surroundings they frequent. This may seem complicated now, but in a short time you will be able to spot these characteristics with surprising ease. If you cannot positively identify a bird, use your field notebook to make a record of your sighting and look it up after you have returned.

Study your guide evenings. Browse through it at leisure. Get to know birds before you encounter them in the field. Get to know where to look for them in the guide. This is an important aid to instant recognition in the field.

bird identification

This book is not a book of bird identification; there are any number of other books that do a complete job of this, as listed on page 189. However, for the beginner, included here are a number of drawings and descriptions of the most often seen common birds.

In each case the size of the bird is given. This is from the tip of the beak to the tip of the tail. The common robin is 8½ to 10½ inches long. The common sparrow is 5 to 6¼ inches long. These birds are not shown since they are so familiar to everyone; their sizes are given for comparison with the new birds you will discover.

BALTIMORE ORIOLE (7–8″) Male is fiery orange and black with two white wing bars. Female and young are olive brown, yellow below. Build nest of woven fibers in drooping upper tree branch.

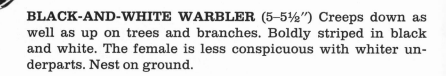

BLACK-AND-WHITE WARBLER (5–5½″) Creeps down as well as up on trees and branches. Boldly striped in black and white. The female is less conspicuous with whiter underparts. Nest on ground.

BLACK-CAPPED CHICKADEE (4¾–5½″) Usually plump. The only small bird with a black cap, a black bib and white cheeks. Friendly and active. The call is a chick-a-dee-dee-dee or dee-dee-dee.

BLUE JAY (11–12″) A large bright blue bird, whitish below with bars on wings. Has a crest and black bib. Very noisy and conspicuous most of the year. Usually travel in groups from 4 to 5.

BROWN CREEPER (5–5¾″) A brown bird smaller than a sparrow with a slender curved bill and rather stiff tail used as a prop. Climbs tree like a spiral staircase then flies to base.

BROWN THRASHER (10½–12″) A slim bird slightly larger than a robin. Is bright rufous-red above and heavily striped below in long stripes. Has wing bars, a curved bill and a long tail.

CARDINAL (8–9″) Easily recognized since it is the only all-red bird with a crest. The male has a black spot at base of bill. The female is yellow-brownish with a touch of red. Red bill.

CATBIRD (8½–9¼″) Slimmer and smaller than the robin. Slate-gray in color with a black cap. Has chestnut red spot under tail coverts not noticeable in the field. Has a mewing song note.

CEDAR WAXWING (6½–8″) A sleek, brown, crested bird, between a sparrow and a robin in size. Black mask over the eyes. Has a broad, yellow band at the tip of the tail. Gentle.

COMMON GOLDFINCH (5–5½″) The male in summer is the only small yellow bird with black wings. Female in summer is dull olive yellow with blackish wings and wing bars. Flight is very undulating.

EASTERN BLUEBIRD (6½–7½″) Larger than a sparrow. The only blue bird with a red breast. Females are paler and duller in color. Many factors have made the Bluebird a favorite over the country.

FLICKER (13–14″) Has wide black crescent across breast, red patch on nape. Conspicuous white rump as the bird flies. The yellow underwing and tail give it a golden color in flight.

CRESTED FLYCATCHER (8–9″) The only flycatcher with a rufous or red colored tail. Has a gray throat and breast and the belly is yellow. Note is a whistled wheeeeep! rising inflection.

25

EASTERN KINGBIRD (8½–9″) A large black and white flycatcher. When it flies the conspicuous wide white band at the tip of its fanlike tail is its best identification mark. Likes fence posts.

PHOEBE (6½–7″) Has no wing bars or eye ring. Gray brown above and whitish below. Constantly wags its tail. The bill is black. Has an upright posture. Repeated call is: "phoe-bee."

WOOD PEWEE (6–6½″) Sparrow-sized flycatcher olive brown above and whitish below with two very conspicuous wing bars but no eye ring. Lower mandible of bill is yellow. Call: "pee-a-wee."

EVENING GROSBEAK (7½–8½″) Large, chunky, short-tailed. Dusky yellowish color and extremely large conical white bill. Male has yellow mask above eyes, black and white wings. Female silver gray.

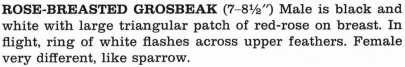

ROSE-BREASTED GROSBEAK (7–8½″) Male is black and white with large triangular patch of red-rose on breast. In flight, ring of white flashes across upper feathers. Female very different, like sparrow.

HOUSE WREN (4½–5¼″) Very small bird in gray-brown color. Has energetic actions and cocks in tail over its back. Has no facial striping as other wrens have. Very songful. Builds in house.

INDIGO BUNTING (5¼–5¾″) The only bird that is a bright deep, rich blue all over. The female is plain brown with no distinctive markings. Male becomes brown in fall but there is some blue.

KINGFISHER (11–14″) Slate-blue head and back. Bushy crest, large head and large beak. Breast is banded in russet. Voice is a high rattle. Nests in tunnels dug in river banks.

MEADOW LARK (9–11″) Yellow breast and under part with black "V" on front of neck. Outer tail feathers are white. Chunky light brown bird. Nests in grass.

MOURNING DOVE (11–13″) A small brown pigeon slimmer than the domestic pigeon. Has a pointed, not fan-shaped, tail which shows large white dots in flight. Call a mournful: ooah, coo, coo, coo.

MYRTLE WARBLER (5–6″) Has a bright yellow rump. Call is a loud "check." Male in spring is blue-gray above, white below, with heavy inverted "U" in black on breast and sides. Female muted.

PURPLE FINCH (5½–6¼″) More old rose or raspberry in color. Rosy-red, brightest on head and rump. Has a large stout bill. The female is heavily striped brown with whitish line over eye.

27

RED-WINGED BLACKBIRD (7½–9½″) Absolutely unmistakable. Black bird with bright red shoulder epaulettes. Female and young are brownish with sharp pointed bill and well defined stripes below.

RUBY-CROWNED KINGLET (3¾–4½″) Tiny, short-tailed olive gray with two pale wing bars and conspicuous broken eye ring. Male has scarlet crown-patch usually concealed. Stubby tail.

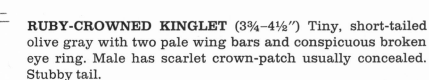

SCARLET TANAGER (6½–7½″) A bright scarlet bird with black wings and tail. The winter male, the immature and the female are dull green above and yellowish below. Males moult in fall season.

SLATE-COLORED JUNCO (6–6½″) Also called Snowbird. Dark slate-gray with white belly. Has conspicuous white outer tail feathers visable in flight. Some have darker hoods. Young are even colored gray.

CHIPPING SPARROW (5–5½″) A small clear, gray-breasted sparrow with a bright rufous cap and a black line through the eye. Almost domestic. Nests near houses. Adults in winter are dull in color.

SONG SPARROW (5–6¾″) Heavily streaked breast with a big "stick pin" or large central spot. Most common eastern sparrow. As it flies, it pumps its tail. Young do not have central spot.

WHITE-THROATED SPARROW (6½–7″) Gray breasted with a white throat patch, a striped black and white crown and a yellow spot between the bill and eye. White-crowned is similar but without throat patch.

BARN SWALLOW (6–7½″) The only swallow with a real "swallow tail." Has white spots on tail, pinkish or cinnamon-buff below and blue-black back. Makes nests of mud in buildings and porches.

PURPLE MARTIN (7½–8½″) Our largest swallow and the only one with a black belly. The male is blue-black above and below, the female is light-bellied. Breed in man-made bird houses.

TREE SWALLOW (5–6″) Steely blue-black or green-black above with immaculate white under-parts. These are the swallows that gather in great flocks on telephone wires late in summer.

TUFTED TITMOUSE (6–6½″) The only gray, mouse-colored bird that has a tufted crest. Its flanks are rusty-colored. Similar to the chickadee but is more wary and flighty. Clear whistle.

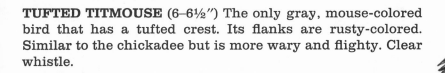

WHITE BREASTED NUTHATCH (5–6″) Descends trees head down. Black beady eye on white cheek. Has black cap, white below with blue back and wings. Similar species is Red Breasted, has eye stripe.

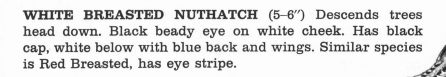

29

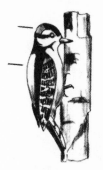

HAIRY AND DOWNY WOODPECKERS (8½–9½″ and 6½–7″ respectively) Are identical except size. White-backed with checkered black and white body. Small red patch on back of head. Females no patch.

RED-BELLIED WOODPECKER (9–10½″) The only zebra striped back woodpecker. Male has entire crown in bright red, female has red on nape of neck only. The young have a brown head, striped body.

RED-HEADED WOODPECKER (8½–9½″) The only bird with entirely red head. In flight, large square patches of white show on rear edge of wing. Male and female are alike, young are dusky.

YELLOW-BELLIED SAPSUCKER (8–8½″) The only woodpecker with a red forehead patch. Has longitudinal white stripe on black wing. Males have red throats; females, white. Young are sooty.

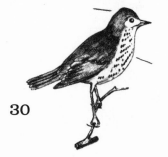

WOOD THRUSH (7½–8½″) Smaller than a robin. Is rust- or rufous-headed with breast and sides heavily spotted. Round spots, not stripes. Similar to Thrasher but Thrush has redder head.

identification by voice

In many cases hearing a bird is just as important as seeing it—sometimes it is even more important. As you get more proficient, you will find that the only way to positively identify some birds is by their voices. For example, the cardinal has five or six different songs or calls. Here is where the advice of a veteran bird watcher comes in handy. On a field trip the experienced watcher will ask the group or individual to be quiet and listen to the voices of the birds. You will be surprised how by careful listening you will hear things that you have never heard before. A set of hi-fi records of all the common bird songs and voices will be helpful. As you get to know birds by their voices, you will know what to look for when you hear a bird call or song.

the bird census

Just as we take the census of people, an effort is made each year to obtain statistics with regard to the bird population. This has been going on for more than 60 years and is known as the Christmas Count since it is taken eight hours a day during ten days or so including Christmas and New Year of each year. The results are tabulated and presented in the Christmas issue of the Audubon Field Notes.

The operation is governed by strict rules and is conducted under the auspices of the National Audubon Society, 1130 Fifth Avenue, New York, N. Y. 10028, and the United States Fish and Wildlife Service, Department of Interior, Washington, D. C. By writing to these organizations you can get pertinent information. Before you do this it will be well to check on possible bird clubs in your area. If there are any, they will have all the plans made for the count and you can work with them.

From these counts, together with data on weather, food supply, and other variable information, much has been learned about the distribution of individual bird species. A better understanding of the requirements of birds is also gained so that better protection can be provided to increase the bird population.

Bird study gives parents and children a valuable common interest.

Participating in this important annual census is a valuable contribution to conservation and the science of ornithology and you will find your efforts well rewarded.

In addition to the annual Christmas Count, there are a number of other counts. While they are of less significance, they are just as interesting and enjoyable.

the big day

The Big Day is a 24-hour bird count taken from midnight to midnight usually during the height of the spring migration. The object of this count is to see how many different species of birds can be sighted during this period. This is definitely a group activity. If the group or club is large, it may break up into smaller divisions, each covering a special location such as highlands, open fields, heavy woods, marshes, river banks, and lakeshores. If the group is small, the participants can travel together to cover the best places during the given time.

the big morning

Sometimes the members of a bird club cannot spare the time for an all-day outing. They then may cut down the Big Day to just a morning in which as many species as possible are identified. This half-day count can also be held in the afternoon if need be.

the small day

The small day usually takes place over a 24-hour period but instead of seeing how many birds can be identified the goal here is to study a few birds in much greater detail. This is very rewarding because it provides an excellent opportunity for firsthand acquaintance with the habits, movements, and general way of life of the few birds you have chosen for study. It means, too, that you do not have to cover so much territory but can choose two or three choice spots and divide your time leisurely between them.

bird photography

This phase of bird watching has many rewards and offers the greatest challenge this hobby can provide. Taking pictures of birds is not a simple task; it requires a vast reserve of patience and ingenuity. Long waits are sometimes necessary before a bird or birds get into the right position and light for a good picture. And it takes ingenuity to get close enough so that a bird can be seen in a picture. If you have never taken pictures before, your first results may fail to satisfy you. Even if you have had some experience with photography, you will have to sharpen your wits and skills.

Those who intend to practice bird photography would do well to obtain a copy of Hunting with the Camera by A. D. Cruickshank. This is one of the best books on the subject. It will eliminate needless experimentation and get you off to a good start in this engaging skill.

While you may already own a camera that can be used for bird photography, special equipment is required. The ordinary 35mm. camera lens is much too small and must be used in conjunction with a quality telephoto lens as shown in the accompanying illustration. The camera in the photograph is installed on a specially made gunstock-type mount which allows the camera to be held very still and rigid. Discuss your plans with your dealer. He may be able to give you valuable advice.

For purposes of convenience, two general types of bird pictures can be distinguished; field pictures and controlled-location pictures.

field pictures

On field trips you will want a light camera of the type illustrated so that you can shoot fast and with a minimum of motion required for adjustments. Birds are extremely fast and you must be ready at all times to take pictures. Remember that any sudden motion will scare them away. When you spot a bird, freeze in position; then walk slowly toward it without sideward motion. Rest at intervals and get as close as possible. It is amazing how large birds appear to the naked eye and how small they become when you get them into your range finder. Nor does their protective coloration make your task easier. Take your picture as quickly as possible. If you wait for just the right pose, you may end up with no picture at all. You will have to build up your collection of photographs by taking the picture available and then replacing the poorer ones with better shots later on.

controlled-location pictures

Perhaps the most interesting and the best pictures are made where the location is controlled as on a feeder or birdbath. When you are attracting birds to your yard with feed and water, you have an excellent opportunity for taking good pictures. Here you have a prearranged setting that will enable you to locate your camera for the best lighting and composition. The camera can be mounted on a tripod close enough to your subjects so that their images will be large and clear like some of the pictures in this book. If the birds seem to be frightened and stay away from the feeder, substitute some object that resembles the camera and keep it in place for several days, if necessary, to

You can combine hobbies such as photography with bird watching.

34

gain their confidence. The camera can be operated by remote control; use a black fishline and small staples to run the line to the place where you are concealed. This same setup can be used for taking pictures of nesting and feeding, but be sure not to disturb the birds or they will leave the nest and not return. When taking pictures in this manner, you can get sharp prints without a telephoto lens.

Another controlled-location type of picture can be made in the field but this requires a great deal of hunting to find a suitable site and careful preparation beforehand. For this setup you can build a regular hunter's blind that will house you and your equipment. This is an excellent way to get pictures of waterfowl. The best blind is the portable type, made of aluminum poles and a dark green canvas cover that can be moved as often as necessary without causing unnecessary disturbance.

For field photography it is best to wear dark-colored clothes so that you are as inconspicuous as possible. You and your equipment should not contrast with the surroundings.

bird banding

Bird banding is a method of labeling birds to learn more about their migration patterns, nesting and wintering habits, and longevity. Small aluminum bands are numbered and attached by bird banders to a bird's leg. The number of each band is recorded and sent, with a record of the estimated age of the bird and the conditions under which it was found, to the central banding office in Laurel, Maryland. Whenever a banded bird is recaptured or found dead, a report is sent to this office and recorded. To date, almost 12,000,000 birds have been banded.

Bird banders set up a very fine black nylon net about ten feet high and forty feet wide. This is placed in a known flyway, and as the birds are trapped, they are taken from the net, a band is placed on the leg, and a record is made. Then the bird is released. Contrary to what some people believe, the netting of birds does not harm them—at most their feathers and dignity are ruffled a bit. Special wire-netting traps are erected on streams and ponds. Some of these traps are quite elaborate.

Bird banding is usually considered work for the advanced student or ornithologist. It is included here, however, because it is an important aspect of bird watching. There are only a few thousand banders in the entire country, so you can see how specialized a field it is. However, more banders can be used, and this work may be of special interest to you. Bird banding is serious business. Before anyone can put a band on a bird's leg he must obtain a permit from the Fish and Wildlife Service of the United States Department of the Interior, a state permit, and be found qualified to do the work. For complete information on this important branch of bird watching, write to the Fish and Wildlife Service, Department of the Interior, Washington, D.C. They will tell you how to get a copy of Manual for Bird Banding written by F. C. Lincoln.

bird migration studies

Another interesting scientific branch of bird watching is the study of bird migration. This is an intriguing subject, and you will find many books in your library on the subject. For more than fifty years the U.S. Fish and Wildlife Service and the Audubon Society have been collecting data on migration. The phenomenon of bird migration is so important that the Migratory Bird Treaty Act has been passed protecting those species which pass back and forth between the United States, Canada, and Mexico. For active participation, get in touch with your local bird club or contact the Audubon Society or the Fish and Wildlife Service in Washington, D. C. An excellent detailed study, Migration of Birds, circular 16, can be obtained from the Superintendent of Documents, Government Printing Office, Washington, D.C.

rare bird alert

A favorite activity of many groups is the Rare Bird Alert. Members of a bird group decide what they believe to be a rare bird or species for the area. As soon as one is identified, they alert the other members to be on the lookout for it. A certain amount of ingenuity is demanded but it's a big thrill to get on the trail of the rare bird.

These group activities are enjoyed immensely by all who take part in them. It has been said that if you meet a person in the country or in a park with a pair of binoculars strung around his neck you need no introduction; you just start to talk since you are on common ground!

bird lists

Bird lists have already been mentioned under "Equipment Needed" where it was suggested that the beginner make an entry in a small notebook of all the birds he identifies. The list can be kept from year to year and can constitute a complete record of your activities, making it possible for you to compare your annual findings. Make the entries as complete as possible: the species, where found, date, the time of day, kind of day, other birds in the vicinity, weather, what it was feeding on, where it was nesting, and any other observations you think significant. Consult with others and see what notes they deem important. In addition to the field notebook, some bird watchers enter their on-the-spot observations in a permanent notebook for handy reference.

a few precautions

A word of caution is necessary at this point. By nature, birds are very suspicious. They do not develop trust in man overnight: it takes time to get them to know you and you will have to be patient with them.

Remember, too, that birds are easily frightened. Any noise or sudden motion will put them to flight. Of the two disturbances, noise and motion, they are more easily frightened by motion. Therefore you must move slowly in the yard and garden. Noise, however, does drive birds away too. Keep things quiet and go about your work slowly and the birds will stay.

You cannot, of course, have cats running at large and hope that the birds will be at ease. Cats and birds just don't go together and you must make up your mind at the start which you would rather have. It seems that dogs do not interfere too much but they too should be kept in control in the bird garden.

bird watching in urban areas

It is generally assumed that the city dweller has little or no chance to do any bird watching or feeding. This is especially true of those who live in apartment houses. Most people believe one must live in the country or in a heavily wooded area to enjoy this hobby.

This is not necessarily the case. True, some bushes and trees must grow in the vicinity to attract the birds in the first place, but once they know that food is available you will be surprised how far they will come to get it. A friend of ours lives in an area of apartment houses. There is not a tree or bush within several blocks of his apartment. However, three blocks away is a park, containing a stream and some bushes and trees, that makes a nice habitat for birds. My friend placed a feeder on his apartment-house window sill, hoping to lure birds from the park, but for several weeks nothing happened. Then one day a common sparrow found the feeder. In a few days there were more sparrows. Now the owner has regular customers of sparrows, chickadees, a pair of cardinals, and, occasionally, other birds.

Do not become discouraged if birds do not appear at once. It may take weeks and weeks before they find the handout, but once they do, you will have to be ready to keep the feeder filled.

We have noticed that if we are away for several weeks and, because of our absence we have not fed the birds, it may take three or four days after our return before the birds are back at the feeders again. Although birds are not the most intelligent of animals, they do seem to form very strong habits that guide and control most of their activities. If they form a habit of coming to your feeder they will continue to come, until you stop putting out food. But once you stop feeding them, you must invite them back again if you want to have them develop the habit of visiting.

Shown on page 82 is a window-shelf feeder that works exceptionally well in an urban area. If you want, you can add a small cup or container for water, such as a tin can, cut down to about an inch and a half high.

An everyday scene on Milwaukee's lake front where mallards and other wild waterfowl gather by the thousands each day. This is an example of how wild birds can be enticed into the heart of a big busy city and enjoy it.

Milwaukee Journal Photo

Again, remember—birds are not fussy. If this feeder is too complicated or you cannot build it, just fasten an ordinary board with a little ridge around it to keep the seeds from falling off to the window sill, and you will certainly find some birds to greet you at your window.

want to start a bird club?*

The approach to starting a club is not the important thing; interest and enthusiasm are the requirements. It takes only two people with a love of nature to start a club, and that club may be as formal or informal as you like.

Start with a few people and meet informally. Take a few field trips and have a few trial meetings before you go any further. When you are ready to broaden your group, ask your local newspaper to publish the fact. Have a meeting in some accessible place with a good speaker and see who shows up. Don't worry in the least about getting a large number of people. It is far, far better to begin building with a small group of enthusiastic workers than to launch your club with several hundred men and women who drop out after the first month.

After two or three meetings with a temporary chairman you ought to know enough to make permanent plans. A sensible procedure at this point is to draft a constitution.

Article One of the constitution usually specifies the name of the club. Every bird club that I am familiar with is named either after an individual prominent in ornithology or after the area that the club will serve. Let your name denote your function. If you are going in for serious scientific study, use the six-syllable word and name yourself an "ornithology" society. But if you are to be just a congenial group of friends who promote conservation and take an occasional bird walk, call yourself simply a "bird club." Many clubs have found it a great advantage to become branches of the National Audubon Society. The name has wide appeal and commands community respect and serves as an attraction to speakers for local programs.

Article Two will explain your purpose. What are you trying to do? Have a social group interested in good fellowship? Improve your own knowledge of wildlife? Engage in scien-

---

* By Louis C. Fink. Condensed by special permission from Audubon Magazine.

tific studies? Educate children? Are you interested in just birds or in all wildlife? Make it clear in your purpose.

Article Three is delegated to membership. May anyone join? How old shall they be? Most clubs provide for student memberships at reduced rates, particularly if they are in a college town where the students may be doing good ornithology research.

Article Four covers meetings. It is normally the custom to meet once a month. The larger clubs have a tendency to meet in public libraries or schools, usually on a public transportation line. Smaller clubs meet in private homes. There should be a provision for an annual meeting.

Article Five should provide for the election of a board of directors. Personally my choice is to have a "Board" which carries on most of the business affairs so your club meetings can hear a few simple reports and vote on just the major issues. All reports should be in writing to save meeting time. Officers are the routine ones: chairman of the board, president, vice-president, secretary, and treasurer. A program committee is essential to success. There must be a meeting place, a speaker, a film, or topic for discussion. It's an excellent idea to have sizable committees to share the burden.

Other Suggestions. I heartily recommend a bulletin, even a simple mimeograph job. It should contain a list of birds seen in your area that month; a notice of next month's meeting and field trips; and some hints of birds to come in the next season.

School and garden clubs will ask you for speakers. As you accumulate funds, plan to buy some bird slides from the National Audubon Society. Bird study will be more fun—and your club stronger—if you affiliate with state and national organizations.

A word about indoor meetings. Keep the business portion as short as possible. Strike a balance between pure entertainment and pure study but don't ignore either. I think it is a mistake to have "refreshments" at every meeting. It is too easy for a bird club to become nothing but a social organization. In that event your good birders will drop out and the social-minded members left will not do much bird study or conservation.

Your leading members can give talks on bird identification. Someone else can discuss bird books (with the help of your local library) and binoculars. If you have any biologists in the area, ask them to talk on the coloration of birds and other subjects. For entertainment consider films from the National Audubon Society, the U. S. Fish and Wildlife Service, individuals, state game commissions, national and state parks, etc.

plantings that attract birds

Plantings perform three functions in a bird-attraction program. First, they supply an additional source of food. The seeds and the fruits of trees, shrubs, vines, and flowers are the natural food of birds. The insects that attack these plantings are also excellent food. Second, plantings offer a place for nesting. In general, birds will prefer natural facilities for building their nests and will use them if available. Third, dense plantings of the right kind give the cover the birds need for protection from their natural enemies.

Well-planned plantings will result in a better landscaped yard and will attract more birds. Try to duplicate nature as closely as possible, so that there will be both open and dense areas. Different foliage attracts different species of birds. The more varied your plantings are, the better will be your chances of attracting a variety of birds.

Locate trees toward the rear, put shrubs and vines in front of them, and then flowers for ground cover. See your local nursery for guidance in selecting what you need and for planning your layout.

Be sure that your planting layout provides for the strategic location of birdhouses, birdbaths, and feeders. If your lot is large enough, include a nature trail. With a little plan-

An open space with trees and shrubs in a natural setting makes an ideal place for attracting birds.

41

ELM

ning you can have a secluded path even on a small lot. A few open spots along the way will surely be a favorite retreat of the birds. The following pages give a list of the more popular trees, shrubs, vines, and flowers.

popular trees that attract birds

ALDER A small tree or bush that is good for mass planting. Provides fair cover for protection but is not used by birds for nesting. Produces a fruit in August and September that is eaten by over 20 species of birds such as the tree sparrow, bobwhite, pheasant, grouse, woodcock, and mourning dove.

AMERICAN ELM An excellent tree for landscape use. Grows up to 129 feet tall. Provides good nesting and is excellent for swinging nests such as those of the oriole. Produces a winged nut seed in March and May that is eaten by the goldfinch, pine siskin, and others. Insects in the bark are eaten by vireos and warblers.

ASH Grows up to 120 feet. Not too good for city planting. Provides good nesting and some protection. Has winged seed in October and November eaten by the purple finch, grossbeak, and bobwhite.

BASSWOOD OR LINDEN Excellent for shade planting. Grows up to 110 feet tall. Has beautiful shape, grows fast, and provides good nesting and protective coverting. In August to October it has a nutlike fruit eaten by many birds such as the redpoll, bobwhite, and grouse. Insects in the bark are eaten by warblers, vireos, and others.

BEECH A large ornamental tree not common in city yards; more suited to its natural surroundings. Provides good nesting facilities and protective cover. A three-angled nut is produced in September and October that is eaten by woodpeckers, blackbirds, flickers, wood duck, blue jays, and others.

ASH

BIRCH Has excellent landscape value and offers good nesting. Decayed limbs are used by woodpeckers and chickadees. Has a small seed in late summer that appeals to the titmouse, junco, finch, and blue jay. Insects that infest the tree are eaten by the warblers and vireos.

CHERRY—BLACK, CHOKE, AND RED (WILD) Not too ornamental and grow best in the wild state. Other trees provide more protection and are better for nesting. Excellent for food. Their fruit (the cherry) attracts over 80 species of birds.

BALSAM FIR Excellent in the wild state and in rural areas. Will not do well in the city because smoke and gases affect it. Provides excellent cover and nesting both in winter and summer. Seeds are in cones which ripen in September and provide food all winter if retained. The seeds are eaten by the robin, waxwing, grouse, thrushes, and other northern birds.

CHOKE CHERRY

FLOWERING CRAB A very attractive tree for lawn planting. Has rose-colored flowers in May. The larger trees provide good protective covering and good nesting. The small fruit is excellent for winter feeding and attracts such birds as the mockingbird, grosbeak, finch, and crossbills and the game birds.

FLOWERING DOGWOOD A favorite ornamental tree, suitable for small or large plantings. Offers a fair amount of cover and the robin and vireo will nest in it. Its red berries are eaten after they are softened by frost. Attracts over 90 species of birds so it is one of the most popular trees with bird fanciers.

HACKBERRY Not an ornamental tree; best suited for wild planting. Fair for cover and nesting. Available the entire winter, its berries are eaten by cardinals, thrashers, waxwings, and over 45 other species.

HAWTHORN A very attractive and popular ornamental tree that is one of the best for landscape value and bird attracting. The thorny, thick growth provides excellent cover and nesting. The thorn apples are eaten by birds all winter. Over 35 species eat the fruit including the bobwhite, thrushes, and grouse.

MAPLES There are many varieties all of which have good landscape value. The dense foliage gives good cover and nesting facilities. A winged nut seed is produced in summer that appeals to over 15 species of birds including nuthatches, robins, and song sparrows.

RED MAPLE

MOUNTAIN ASH Excellent for ornamental planting but not very good for nesting and cover. The red and orange berries provide fall and winter food for robins, waxwings, woodpeckers, and orioles.

43

MULBERRY

RED OAK

SPRUCE

MULBERRY Its graceful, light-green foliage makes it a good tree for ornamental planting and provides good coverage and nesting. Its soft, juicy fruit is eaten during the early summer and the entire nesting season. Attracts over 40 species of birds including cardinals, catbirds, thrushes, and mockingbirds.

NORWAY SPRUCE One of the most popular of the ornamental trees, often planted to provide a wind break. Excellent for nesting and cover. The cones have seeds that are eaten by finches, grouse, grosbeaks, and other birds.

OAK (RED) Excellent for ornamental planting but grows very slowly up to 150 feet tall. Good for nesting and protection. Produces acorns, which are eaten by almost all species of birds. The insects that infect the bark are also eaten by birds. Almost all oaks possess these characteristics. The Northern Red Oak is found from Maine to Minnesota.

RED CEDAR Over 30 species are known and most of them are used extensively for ornamental planting. Provides a year-round shelter and is good for nesting. The purple-blue berries ripen in early fall and provide food throughout the entire winter. Attract all the native birds that inhabit the eastern half of the country.

SHADBUSH A small tree that has white blossoms in May. Offers only fair cover and nesting facilities. In midsummer it produces red berries that are eaten by over 50 species of birds, which makes it a favorite for attracting birds.

SOUR GUM An unusual tree that has brilliant colors in fall. Provides good cover and nesting. Its blue berries last well into winter and are eaten by wood ducks, woodpeckers, thrushes, waxwings, blue jays, pheasants, robins, and many other beneficial birds.

WHITE PINE Its fine height makes it excellent for background planting. It provides excellent cover, good nesting for finches, siskins, and warblers, and good roosting for owls. Its cones provide abundant seed for food. Attracts bobwhites, woodpeckers, pine siskins, nuthatches, warblers, and many other birds.

WHITE SPRUCE Grows tall and is very beautiful. Has fine landscape value and provides excellent cover and nesting. The cones bear seed that are eaten by crossbills, finches, chickadees, woodpecks, and over 20 other species.

44

popular shrubs that attract birds

ARROWWOOD Excellent for mass planting. Grows up to 15 feet high and provides good nesting and cover. Produces a blue berry in early fall that is eaten by birds migrating south. Attracts flickers, catbirds, bluebirds, and more than 30 other species.

ASIATIC SWEETLEAF A fine, showy bush for single planting. With only fair nesting and cover qualities, it is better known for its food value. Has a beautiful blue berry sought by birds during the fall. Attracts vireos, robins, and almost all other songbirds.

BAYBERRY Not too attractive for landscape use and only fair for nesting and cover. However, it is the best bird food producer in the eastern states with its fruit which lasts through the entire winter. Attracts more than 75 species of birds, including all the native species.

BLACKHAW Grows 20 feet high singly or in groups. Provides good nesting and cover. Has a blue-back berry that lasts through the winter .Woodpeckers, waxwings, thrushes eat it, as do more than 30 other species.

BLACK HUCKLEBERRY Has fair landscape value and is quite attractive in the fall. Provides fair cover but no nesting to speak of. Fruit is available for a short time during the summer only and is a favorite for more than 45 species of birds such as grosbeaks, towhees, bluebirds, robins, chickadees, and catbirds.

BUCKTHORN

BUCKTHORN Makes a good hedge and provides fair to good nesting and cover. Has a black fruit in late summer and early fall that is eaten by both song and game birds such as grouse, pheasants, finches, thrashers, and waxwings.

BURNING BUSH A good landscape bush in the Midwest that grows from 6 to 10 feet high. It provides fair cover. The seeds ripen in October and stay on the bush until midwinter. Fruit is flame colored. It is eaten by 15 species including grouse and pheasant in late fall.

CORALBERRY Fine for mass planting. Provides good cover and excellent nesting for sparrows. The coral-colored berries ripen in late summer and stay on the branches through winter. They are eaten by both song and game birds.

45

DOGWOODS There are many varieties all of which have good landscape value in the flowering season and some of which are very beautiful with their yellow or red stems in the winter. Afford good protection and fair nesting, especially in the wild state. In September a blue-white berry is formed that is available to birds until midwinter. Favored by all birds.

DOGWOOD

ELDERBERRY Good for mass planting and as a wild shrub. Can be seen along country roadsides. Gives good cover and nesting. The juicy black fruit ripens in late summer and early fall and is eaten by over 115 species of birds which makes it a natural for the bird garden.

HIGHBUSH CRANBERRY Has exceptionally fine flowers, foliage, and fruit and is recommended by the Soil Conservation Service. Its fine growth provides good nesting and excellent cover. The fruit ripens in September and October and lasts through the winter. Eaten by game birds but only a few songbirds.

HIGHBUSH BLUEBERRY A thick well-shaped shrub that has excellent fall foliage. It has good cover and fair nesting qualities. The fruit is the market variety of blueberry that ripens in midsummer. The berries are eaten by over 90 species of birds.

HONEYSUCKLE Almost a vine in shape. Provides good cover and nesting. The crimson berry ripens in fall and is available until early winter. It is eaten by birds while migrating. Almost all songbirds feed on the berry.

ELDERBERRY

INKBERRY An evergreen shrub that has fine landscape use. Mass planting provides good cover. Produces a black berry that is the winter food of many birds such as the chickadee, titmouse, bobwhite, bluebird, robin, and catbird.

JAPANESE BARBERRY A widely used ornamental shrub that may be trimmed into hedges. Its sharp thorns provide excellent protection and good nesting for birds. Has a red berry that serves as an emergency food during winter. Eaten by sparrows, juncos, catbirds, thrushes, and many others.

MAPLE-LEAVED VIBURNUM Excellent for low mass plantings—very popular with nurserymen. Good for ground nesting birds such as grouse. Affords fine cover and produces fruit in fall for winter feeding. Attracts the flicker, robin, grouse, bobwhite, waxwing, bluebird, and others.

46 *HIGH BUSH CRANBERRY*

NANNYBERRY Has white flowers and black berries and is fine for mass plantings. It provides both nesting and cover. Its fruit is the staple winter food for grouse, pheasant and many songbirds.

PASTURE ROSE Grows 3 feet high and is fine for mass planting in wild gardens and woods. The strong, stiff spines provide the best possible protection for birds. It is used by some low-nesting birds. The red berry is available all winter and enjoyed by some 40 species of birds.

SAND CHERRY A low-growing bush hardly over 3 feet high. Wants sandy soil. Has only fair nesting and coverage qualities. The red-purple berry ripens in August and is related to the choke cherry. Provides food for almost all song and game birds.

SNOWBERRY A good shrub for border planting in masses with good nesting and protective qualities. The white fruit stays on the branches all winter. Over 30 species eat the fruit.

WILD RASPBERRY (RED AND BLACK) Best in wild surroundings; does not have good landscape value. The thick growth and the thorny spines make it excellent for protection and nesting. Late summer produces the red and black raspberries that are eaten by over 100 species of birds.

WINTERBERRY Has good landscape value: grows 5 to 10 feet high and has fine flowers and scarlet berries. Has both nesting and cover qualities. The scarlet berries ripen in September and stay on the branches well into winter thus providing natural food for both song and game birds.

WITHE ROD A very good landscape bush with showy-white flowers and varicolored berries. Provides good nesting and cover. Berries last into winter and are eaten by over 35 species of birds.

popular vines that attract birds

BITTERSWEET A very popular vine with red-orange berries that are attractive not only outdoors but in the house as well. Is now protected in public areas and should not be picked. Has good landscape qualities when grown on an

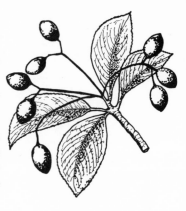

NANNYBERRY

WINTERBERRY

BITTERSWEET

47

arbor. Has no nesting or cover qualities to speak of. The berries are an excellent source of bird food in fall and well into the winter. Eaten by both song and game birds.

MATRIMONY VINE When planted in masses or as a wall covering, it has good landscape value. Vine has strong spines which provide excellent protection and nesting. The scarlet fruit is available in fall and early winter and is eaten by migrating and local songbirds.

GREENBRIER Has little landscape value, but its thick growth gives it good nesting and covering qualities for protecting birds. The fruit is excellent and lasts the entire winter well above the snow line. It is eaten by 50 species.

HALL'S HONEYSUCKLE The flowers are attractive and the vine is used extensively as a wall covering. Affords good winter protection since the leaves stay on. Also provides good nesting. The black berries last well into winter. Such birds as song sparrows, flickers, grouse, and meadow larks feed on them.

VIRGINIA CREEPER Another popular vine used extensively for decoration. Has brilliant color in fall. Provides good cover and nesting. The Virginia Creeper is perhaps the best producer of natural food for birds and should be planted wherever possible.

WILD GRAPE This prolific vine has no landscape value for formal planting but it is a must for the wild garden. It provides only fair cover and nesting but its grapes are the fall and winter diet of almost all birds. This one vine will attract every species of birds.

ground cover planting of flowers

Almost all kinds of flowers provide seed food for birds. Their bright blooms not only attract birds but also beautify the owner's grounds.

In planting flowers as ground cover, locate them in clusters, not as single specimens. Some of the species that are especially desirable for this purpose include princess feather, love-lies-bleeding, sunflowers, bellflower, chrysanthemum, columbine, pinks, cosmos, portulaca, and gaillardia. These can be used for borders along the garden path or in front of the shrub plantings.

If you are making a nature trail, wild flowers ought to be planted along it. To give the right effect, they should be planted in large patches, just the way they grow in nature.

Clusters of asters, black-eyed Susans, blazing star, chicory, and asparagus are suggested. In the typical wild garden, the grass is not cut and no attempt is made to give it that manicured look which marks exclusive residential neighborhoods. Rough and natural surroundings are quite to the liking of birds and provide a natural habitat for them.

food: the first requirement

Of the three essentials for attracting birds—food, water, and shelter—food is the most important. Without food, birds will not flock to any area. There is a direct relationship between the amount of food provided and the number of birds that will settle.

At nesting time birds of the same species will claim territories with boundaries and guard these small areas from any intruder of the same species. Because of this, only a limited number of that species will be found in any locale. But birds of different species will mingle and use the same feeding and watering stations. Birds are invited by suitable houses and nesting facilities, but the finest houses and shelters will not keep birds in your yard if you do not provide enough of the right kind of food.

Birds need huge quantities of food compared to their size. If we all ate "like birds" we would have endless meals that daily almost equaled our own weight. In natural surroundings enough food is usually supplied by trees, vines, plants, and berries. But the average city lot, or even a fair-sized garden or country lot, cannot provide enough food for more than a few birds. Food must be supplied to encourage a high bird population and to attract a variety of birds to the area.

There are two different types of feeding: summer feeding and winter feeding. As the names imply, these feeding methods are dictated by the weather and involve two different procedures. Many people, believe   that they are doing their duty by throwing bread crumbs to birds throughout the year. it is true that they are helping by giving the birds some extra food, but they are not supplying what the birds actually like and need. The person who feeds birds correctly varies their diet according to the time of year.

Many localities have enough food to support a normal number of birds during the summer. But, if an area is lacking in trees, if there are few or no garden spots, if there is little natural or even planted vegetation, then summer feeding is as important as winter feeding if birds are to be attracted and help in the neighborhood.

summer feeding

Summer feeding will naturally bring more birds to the yard and garden. Birds brighten our lives which is reason enough to feed them well. Indeed, summer feeding of birds is a greater benefit to people than to the birds themselves.

With a little patience and time, most birds can be trained to come up to your house. A friend of mine, who has a beautiful home in a well-wooded area on the outskirts of a large city, built an ordinary platform feeder and placed it at the edge of the woods. Here he fed the birds every day. At the end of each week he moved the feeder, which was on a pipe, about 5 to 6 feet closer to the house. The birds scarcely noticed the change of location and day by day came to the feeder, and each week came a little closer to the house. In a short time the feeder was right outside the windows facing the breakfast nook and kitchen. The birds became accustomed to the location, the noise and movements in the house, and the closeness of the people. They were not too easily frightened and seemed to develop confidence in their benefactor. As a result, every day as my friend and his family eat breakfast or lunch or as his wife works in the kitchen, they have an audience of pert little kibitzers looking on. Their songs and antics and their friendliness and trust can be enjoyed not only during the summer but in winter as well and thus they provide year-round entertainment. Although the birds do benefit by the feeder during the winter and actually need it, these people engage in summer feeding primarily for their own enjoyment.

Avoid overfeeding birds in summer. During this time they instinctively look for natural food in the form of weed seeds, insects, and wild berries, and summer feeding may make them too reliant on their unnatural source of food. Summer feeding does give the birds a change of diet which they appreciate. It has another advantage: due to nesting habits, birds are usually scattered over a wide area in summer. Feeding them at this time of the year will sometimes bring more birds into a given area.

winter feeding

Winter feeding is the more important and practical phase of feeding birds. With the arrival of cold weather and snow their natural food becomes scarce. But a warning must be given at this point. Do not start to winter-feed and then give it up. Once feeding is begun, it must be continued; if not, you may be guilty of killing hundreds of birds. Winter feeding makes birds dependent upon man and if it is stopped there is no substitute for this source of supply which has lured the birds from their natural wintering quarters. If you have enticed birds into your "dining room," and invited them to be your guests, you must see them through, and provide for them the entire winter.

A successful winter feeding program must begin early in fall—even late summer is not too soon. As the birds migrate to the south, they will come to your feeders for food, and if

Pacific Flyway

Central Flyway

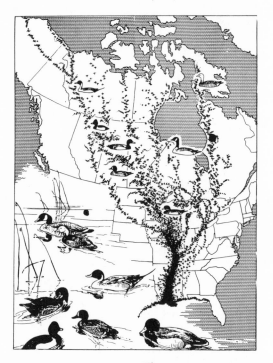

Mississippi Flyway

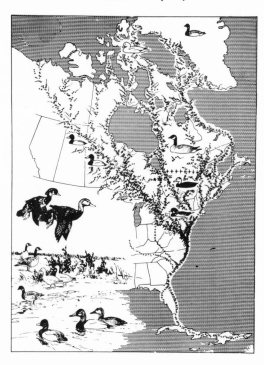

Atlantic Flyway

Here is a map showing the principal migration routes used by ducks and geese that pass through North America to their wintering grounds in the south. Thousands of people all over America helped wildlife biologists determine the routes or flyways used by our waterfowl between their northern nesting grounds and southern wintering areas.

the other facilities are also satisfactory, they may stay over the winter. You will have as your guests birds who normally summer north of your locality and winter south of you. A good winter feeding program will also hold over the winter many of the birds who spend the summer in your area. So, it is possible to have two groups of different types of birds, and since it is not nesting time, you will find that members of the same species will flock together in large numbers.

Begin the feeding in early fall or later summer. Local birds will be the first to become familiar with the facilities and frequent your premises. They will attract migrating birds who will also feed. Gradually the newcomers will become acquainted with the surroundings and adapt themselves to the conditions they find. Then, as the colder weather comes, they will be ready for it.

After your feeding program gets under way, follow through faithfully without missing a single feeding, because the natural food supply has been depleted. Sufficient food and water must be available at all times. Continue feeding through late winter and well into spring when the birds can again eat insects, berries, and seeds.

It would be difficult to give specific information or make promises on the kinds of numbers of birds that you will

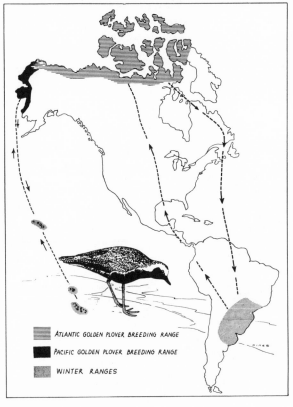

From banding we learned Atlantic Golden Plover returns north over a different route than the one it follows south to its wintering grounds.

ATLANTIC GOLDEN PLOVER BREEDING RANGE

PACIFIC GOLDEN PLOVER BREEDING RANGE

WINTER RANGES

55

attract by winter feeding. Any information that would apply throughout the country would be very general and of little help.

There are many variables such as migration paths and the natural characteristics of the countryside. But by learning the requirements of their own locality, thousands of people are attracting and holding birds each year and for many years.

bird diets

To make a feeding program successful, it is necessary to know the diet of the birds you wish to attract and to duplicate their natural food as closely as possible.

On the basis of their eating habits, birds may be divided for convenience into insect-eating and seed-eating birds, although the distinctions between them is not clean-cut. Since the majority of birds fall into both categories, feeding presents little difficulty as far as variety in their diet is concerned. It is advisable to use separate feeders, some for insects and some for seeds. If you wish, you can have a combination feeder for both types of food, or for the birds that eat both insects and seeds. The more feeders you have the more numerous and varied will be the birds you attract. With several well-located feeders you will provide for the natural tendency of birds to flit about from place to place pecking, scratching, and exploring.

grit—an essential addition

Birds must take a certain amount of grit, usually a very fine sand or gravel, with their food for digestion. In normal, natural feeding, the pecking a bird does on the ground provides this grit. In winter feeding, when birds do not get enough grit this way, it must be added to their food. Usually very fine washed sand or gravel is needed. While it may be purchased, any fine sand that you can find in your locality will work. Watch where an excavation for a new building is being made and if they strike sand, take home a small bag. A little will last all winter. A teaspoon of grit to a quart of feed is sufficient. Crushed charcoal can also be used to provide grit.

suet—a gourmet food

Insect-eating birds eat a large amount of animal matter, mostly insects and their larvae. The best substitute for this fare is ordinary beef suet. Suet is ideal for maintaining the high body temperature of birds, which ranges from 100 to 112 degrees F., and can be obtained inexpensively from your butcher. When buying it, ask for suet that is not stringy, but rather "short." Stringy suet is hard for birds to eat and does not melt down smoothly when rendered to make prepared bird food. You can keep suet without refrigeration and it can be melted and used as needed. All the insect-eating birds love it, and will eat it even if their natural food is available.

Chunks of suet can be tied to a tree notch with string.

how to serve suet

Suet can be served just as you get it from the butcher. You can simply place it on the feeding platform. As the birds peck at it, however, it may fall to the ground, where it will attract rats. One way to hold it in place is to nail it to the platform or to tie a chunk of it to a tree branch.

A better way to serve suet is to make a small basket 3 x 3 x 10 inches out of a ½-inch wire mesh, also known as hardware cloth. This basket can be nailed to a tree or feeder platform. Never nail the basket to any part of your house because the suet will melt, leaving a fat, unsightly stain on the building. Some persons claim that the facilities provided for birds should have no exposed metal surfaces. They believe that if birds come in contact with metal during cold weather, they may freeze to them. I know of no instance where this has happened. But, if desired, the metal parts can be dipped in liquid latex rubber or painted with latex. All metal parts in the feeders described in this book can be treated in this way.

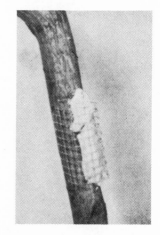

A basket made of wire mesh will hold suet in place.

There are still other ways of serving raw suet. Chunks can be placed in an open mesh bag, such as a potato or onion sack. The bag can then be nailed to a tree or elsewhere.

The best way to serve suet is to build a suet feeder, described in the following pages. These feeders are simple to build, conserve food, and protect it from the weather. Suet combined with various kinds of seeds in cake form keeps longer and has no waste. It is simple and clean to put into the feeders. Also, it is fun to make.

An onion or potato sack is convenient for large chunks.

preparation of suet

Making suet into cakes is simple. First put the suet through an ordinary kitchen food grinder. This will break it up into small pieces and the suet can then be melted down into a smooth mass. If this step is omitted, the suet will stay lumpy and you will not be able to pour it and mix it with

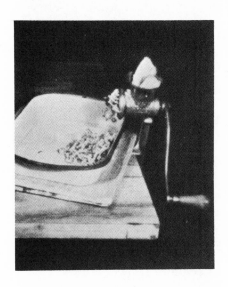

Cut heavy weight aluminum foil into squares.

Make forms by wrapping aluminum around tapered blocks.

the seeds. After the suet is ground, heat in a double boiler. As soon as it has melted, allow it to cool until it hardens.

Do not mix the suet with the seed the first time it is melted. If the suet is allowed to cool and harden, and then is remelted and cooled a second time, it becomes much harder. When remelted pour the suet into the holes in a suet log or into small cake forms made of aluminum foil. You can also use as forms the heavier aluminum foil dishes that frozen foods come in or any other receptacle you have.

Pour twice-melted suet in a semiliquid state over seeds in forms.

suet-seed cakes

Suet-seed cakes are made for birds that eat both insects and seeds and this includes the majority. As the name indicates, the cakes are made of a mixture of seed and suet. There are many satisfactory formulas of suet and seed mixtures. To produce the mixture, add to the melted suet any one or all of the following materials:

Millet	Rice
Sunflower seed	Cracked corn
Raisins	Chopped peanuts
Corn meal	Cooked noodles
Oatmeal	Cooked spaghetti

You may have additional ideas. Why not try to develop your own formula?

To make cakes put the seeds into any of the receptacles or forms described above. Let the suet cool slightly until it begins to set. If the suet is too hot and too runny, some of the seeds will float. If you like, you can pour the semiliquid suet over seeds that you have placed in half-grapefruit shells or in a coconut shell. These can be set out on the feeder platforms in the shells and when empty, refilled.

Two coconut shell feeders, both of which can be used for melted suet and seed, are illustrated on page 102. The one with the entrance hole can be almost filled with the mixture, leaving just enough room for the hungry nuthatches and chickadees to enter. There are many other ways in which suet-seed mixtures can be used to feed birds. You can drop the seed into the melted suet, and when it is in the plastic stage and about to harden, the mixture can be forced into the holes of a log feeder.

Melted suet can be poured over seeds in grapefruit shells, coconut shells, and other forms.

Suet-seed preparations make fine Christmas decorations as well as holiday gifts for the birds. When in the plastic-liquid state, the mixture can be poured over a dead pine bough. (This should not be done on a living tree since the hot suet would kill the branch.) The mixture will stick to the dead branch, which can then be attached to a living tree or used as a winter window-box decoration. When pouring the melted suet, hold another utensil below to catch the drippings, or try dipping the branch into the mixture, but that can be wasteful since some of the seeds and suet will fall to the ground.

For insect eating birds, the National Audubon Society has developed a food mixture called a "food tree" which approximates, rather closely, the bird diet provided by normal insect clusters. This formula was developed by Von Berlepsch and bears his name. The mixture is made as follows:

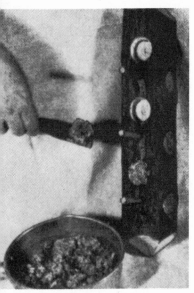

With the suet-seed mixture in a semiliquid state, press it into the holes of your log feeder.

Bread, dried and ground	5 oz.
Meat, dried and ground	3
Hempseed	5
Millet	3
Ant "eggs"	2
Sunflower seed	3
Dried berries	1½

The ingredients are well mixed and then one and one-half times as much melted suet is added. It can be offered to the birds like the suet-seed mixtures. It was originally intended to be put on tree branches and for that reason was called the "food tree." In place of ant eggs, the dried meat can be increased to 5 ounces.

Suet-seed mixture forced into a pine cone or spread on the bark of a tree makes an inviting holiday treat for birds.

peanut butter as bird food

Many birds, especially chickadees, tree sparrows, and juncos, like peanut butter more than suet. Like suet it provides the food values needed to maintain their high body temperature. Peanut butter may be used in place of suet in all of the formulas given above; it can also be spread on the bark of trees or put in the holes of log feeders. Although peanut butter is an excellent food for many of the birds, it is expensive to use for this purpose, since many birds, sometimes hundreds, may frequent winter feeding grounds.

The mixing of seed and kitchen fat is a pleasant pastime and the filling of feeders is an instructive and practical way to get youngsters interested in bird watching and conservation.

fat-seed mixtures

There is no end to the variety of formulas that can be used for preparing bird food. One of the more popular—and a very low-cost mixture—uses kitchen fat. To prepare this, collect discarded kitchen fat in a can or tin cup. When you have a sufficient amount stir into it corn meal or flour or any of the seeds previously described. This will make a rather soft mass because the fat will not harden as suet does. Since it will be used principally for winter feeding, the low outside temperature will keep it firm. It is a good idea to add a little salt to all these mixtures since the birds relish it. The fat-seed mixture, as well as other mixtures, may be spread on the rough bark of trees. This is a natural location for food and birds will enjoy pecking at it there.

seed feeding

Since all birds eat some seeds, seed feeding will attract a large number of them; even predominantly insect-eating birds will turn to seeds in winter when insects are not available. Almost every type of seed is usable and your

Cardinals have a special fondness for sunflower seeds.

local feed store will be able to supply you with many different kinds. Those most readily obtainable include:

Sunflower	Buckwheat
Hempseed	Cracked corn
Millet	Wheat

Add to these such foods as nut meats, ground dog biscuit, chaff, raisins, dried berries, bread crumbs, and even rabbit food, and you have a wide range of food from which to choose. All of these and mixtures made from them have been used successfully to feed and attract birds. A fine balanced mixture that can be made from some of these ingredients is as follows:

Sunflower	30%	Millet	30%
Hempseed	30%	Buckwheat	10%

By varying this formula, you can develop other mixtures. Contact your local feed and seed dealer; he will be glad to help you. He may have a sale on some seed that is overstocked or slightly damaged yet suitable for bird use. One man I know found he could buy at give-away prices peanut butter that did not meet specifications. He now has a source of peanut butter that allows him to use it for all his feeding. Another man gets leftover seed corn and with a homemade grinder does his own grinding and cracking of the corn. The food costs him almost nothing and he is taking care of hundreds of birds.

your own seed mixture

How about experimenting and developing your own exclusive seed mixtures? Here is one way to do it: Mount two aluminum TV dinner trays on a feeding board, as shown. Tack them in place, making sure to puncture the trays so that rain and melted snow will drain out. This compartmentalized arrangement will give you the chance to see what the birds in your yard prefer. In the illustrations, cracked corn, sunflower seeds, commercial bird feed, raisins (much too expensive) and oatmeal were put into separate compartments. If you place the feeder where you can observe it at close range, you can find out what food is eaten first, and what is the birds' preference. However, birds like to scratch, and it is certain that some of the food will be spilled into the ajoining tray area.

You can pass your results on to other bird watchers and in that way help them with their feeding—all of which makes you a sort of expert.

our seed mixture

With all the bird feeding my family has done, we have finally come to a very simple formula. We have found that for this region (lower Wisconsin), the food that birds seem to like most and which attracts the greatest number of them is a 50-50 mixture of sunflower seeds and cracked corn. These are quite inexpensive and available in bag lots. You can usually buy both at a local feed store or grain elevator.

Just a note of warning: when you buy cracked corn, be sure it is cracked and not ground. Cracking breaks up the kernels into good-sized chunks. Ground corn, as the name implies, is ground and in the process a good amount of very fine "flour" is produced that is a complete waste—even squirrels do not seem to like it. If you can only obtain the ground corn that I suggest you sieve it through a piece of common metal window screening. If possible, store the bulk food in metal containers and cover it to keep out spiders and moisture.

commercial seed mixtures

There are many well-balanced seed mixtures on the market which are put up by reputable seed firms. Some of them also prepare the same high-quality mixtures under different names for local department stores, pet shops, and gardeners. These are branded as special for the firm that handles them. The seed mixtures of the leading companies make excellent bird feed, but they are more expensive than home-made preparations made from different types of seed purchased separately. In buying commercial mixes, be sure that they are put out by a reputable firm and note the proportion of seeds in the mixture. Some people have purchased what they thought was a good feed only to find that it was given bulk by the addition of a lot of filler seeds which were not eaten by the birds.

Seed may be spread on the ground by hand but this is wasteful since it becomes covered with snow. It may also attract rats to your yard.

how to seed-feed birds

There are many ways to feed seed to the birds. The simplest, of course, is to spread it on the ground. This method provides natural feeding conditions for birds and they will respond well to it. But the seed may attract animals that are not wanted, such as field mice and rats, and it may also spoil the appearance of your yard. In winter the feed may be covered with snow and quite a bit of seed will be wasted.

There are some birds that prefer to eat off the ground, and to take care of them during the winter, spread canvas or a burlap bag on the ground, holding it in place with wooden pegs at the corners. It can be easily removed for cleaning and the snow removed without difficulty.

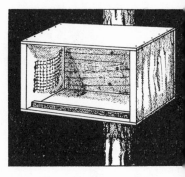

A convenient, low-cost feeder made of an apple box with wire mesh to hold the suet in place and a strip on the front to prevent the seed from falling out. Nail it to a tree or post.

Perhaps the most practical way to feed birds is by feeders such as those shown on the following pages. They are simple to make and vary in design from the simple platform to elaborate window-box types. All of them have been satisfactory. You can select the ones you want to make on the basis of your skill as a craftsman.

The advantages of feeders are many. Grit can be easily added to the food. Then, too, feeders can be cleaned very easily. Since even a small child can tend them, they provide a fine opportunity for the youngsters to take part in your bird-feeding program. Feeders protect birds from their natural enemies, cats and squirrels, since most of them can be mounted on metal poles or wires with shields. In addition, most feeders protect the food from rain and snow.

After a little thoughtful experimenting, you will learn where your feeders can be placed to best advantage. A few hints may help.

For winter feeding, place feeders so that they are sheltered from the north wind. The south or east side of your house or building will provide the most sun and protection. Whenever possible, spot the feeder so that a cat cannot jump on it from a nearby fence or other structure. If the feeder is to be mounted on an upright, put a protective cone-shaped metal shield on it to prevent cats from climbing up, or mount the feeder on an iron pipe. If the feeder is of the hanging type, keep it clear of branches and use a long wire that cats and squirrels cannot negotiate.

While there are advantages in locating feeders away from buildings, it is desirable, especially in winter, to have one near a window where you can watch the birds close at hand and conveniently stock it with food. Much time is saved when you can just open a window and put out the feed for the birds.

Since birds like to flit back and forth from place to place, locate your feeders, if possible, where there are trees such as evergreens, which will provide natural protective cover for them. When they are disturbed, they can fly to cover and feel safe. Also have some object nearby, but not too close, such as a roost, high fence, or large branch of a dead tree that the birds can use as a landing strip to survey the situation before they alight on the feeder. Birds are suspicious and want to see everything about them before they move.

A Suggestion:

It is important that you place your feeders where birds are most likely to come, but it is just as important that they be placed where you can get to them easily. This often is not done. When locating them in the fall, try to visualize what that spot will be like in the middle of winter. Is it where you usually have 4-ft. drifts? Will you normally have a path shoveled to that location? Sometimes feeders are placed where they are inaccessible during the time of the year when birds are in most need of food, with the result that food is never put out for them.

A shock of corn or other grain provides birds with food during winter, a place to hunt and peck, and excellent protection from the weather.

Don Wooldridge—from the National Audubon Society

Make the most of the bird instinct to peck for its food. One of the best methods is to have a large shock of corn-stalks with leaves and ears near the winter feeders. A shock of wheat, oats, or barley can be used but corn is the best because it will afford a high perch from which the birds can view the feeder. In addition, it provides good protection from severe weather, food for hunting and pecking, as well as nesting material in the spring. Locate the shock in a good place and birds will make good use of it throughout the fall, winter, and spring.

suet log feeder

As the name implies, the suet log feeder is made of a log with the bark still adhering to it. To make one, select any type of wood, although a hardwood, such as oak, is preferable. Elm makes very good log feeders because its branches are round and straight. Select a piece 4 inches in diameter, and cut it 19½ inches long. Point the ends at about 45 degrees and drill a ¾-inch hole just below the bevel at the top for the nut of the ¼-inch eye bolt. Always use an eye bolt instead of a screw eye; a screw eye will pull out in time. Drill the vertical ¼-inch hole for the eye bolt in the upper end.

Drill the 1¼-inch holes (or larger) for the suet as indicated. Also drill holes for perches under two opposite rows of suet holes. Drive in the ¼-inch dowel perches.

Oil painted on the top and bottom will help to prevent checking.

Hang the suet log feeder on long wire away from the tree for protection against squirrels. If the feeders swing too much, attach another wire at the bottom with a weight on it.

bill of materials

Log:	4-in. dia. x 19½ in.
Dowels for perches:	6—¼-in. dia. x 2¼ in.
Eye bolt (with nut and washer)	1—¼ x 2½ in.

SUET LOG FEEDER

MADE OF A 4-INCH DIA LOG
POINTED AT BOTH ENDS

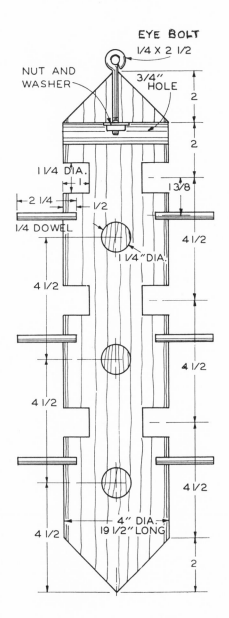

EYE BOLT
1/4 X 2 1/2

NUT AND
WASHER

3/4" HOLE

2

2

1 1/4 DIA.

1

1 3/8

2 1/4

1/2

1/4 DOWEL

1 1/4" DIA.

4 1/2

4 1/2

4 1/2

4 1/2

4 1/2

4 1/2

4" DIA.
19 1/2" LONG

2

69

square-block suet feeder

The square-block feeders are very versatile because they accommodate both the clinging types of birds as well as those that like a perch. Use a piece of wood 4 by 4 (3⅝ by 3⅝) by 18 in. long. Lay the wood out according to the drawing. Bevel the top and bottom 45 deg. and then drill the horizontal ¾-in. hole for the nut of the eye bolt. Do not use a screw eye because it will pull out in time. Drill the 1½-in. holes for holding the suet. On two opposite sides drill the holes for the ¼-in. perches. On the other two opposite sides, make horizontal saw cuts which will serve as footholds for clinging birds. This sawing can be easily done on the circular saw as shown. Drive in the ¼-in. dia. by 2¼-in. dowel perches.

The feeder can be stained brown, but do not paint it. Allow it to weather at least a month before food is put into it. Hang the feeder on long wire away from the tree trunk so that squirrels cannot reach it. If the feeder swings too much, use a wire to attach a weight to the bottom.

bill of materials

Body:	1—4 x 4—18 in.
Dowels for perches:	6—¼-in. dia. x 2¼ in.
Eye bolt (with nut and washer):	1—¼ in. x 2 in.

SUET FEEDER

MADE OF PINE 4 X 4 - 18"LONG

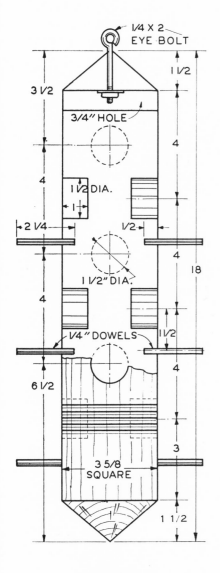

1/4 X 2
EYE BOLT

1 1/2

3 1/2

3/4" HOLE

4

4

1 1/2 DIA.

1

2 1/4

1/2

4

1 1/2" DIA.

18

4

1/4" DOWELS

1 1/2

6 1/2

4

3

3 5/8
SQUARE

1 1/2

PYRAMID TOP
AND BOTTOM

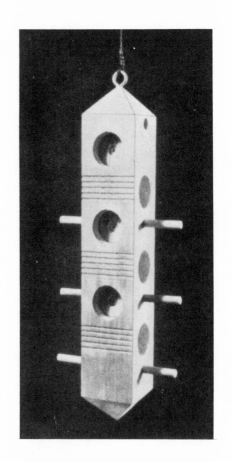

CLING GROOVES ARE CUT
ON CIRCULAR SAW →

71

seed feeder and suet log
turned on a lathe

Anyone with a woodworking lathe can make this practical feeder that is attractive to birds and which is a yard and garden ornament as well. The suet is inserted in the holes in the turned body of the feeder and the seed is put into the circular troughs around the center. It has a place for grit, which is important to birds for digestion. The feeder can be made of any type of wood. Maple is best, although white pine is easy to turn and work.

Make the upright body first. Drill the holes on a drill press if one is available. The top is made of ¾-in. stock. The bottom is made of 2-inch stock. Perhaps you will have to glue up wood for the bottom to obtain the 18-in. diameter.

Drill holes in the body for perches on two sides of the upper holes. Screw the bottom on from below using a 3-in. wood screw. The top can be nailed on the upright body with 2½-in. finishing nails driven at an angle toward the center. A screw eye, 4 in. long, will help to hold the unit together.

The feeder can be painted, if desired, or stained. Allow it to weather before it is put up.

bill of materials

Body: 1—3¼ x 3¼ x 10½ in.
Top: 1— ¾ x 15   x 15   in.
                                 round
Bottom: 1—2   x 18 x 18   in.
                                 round
Dowels for
  perches: 2— ¼-in. dia. x 3   in.
Screw eye: 1—4   in. long

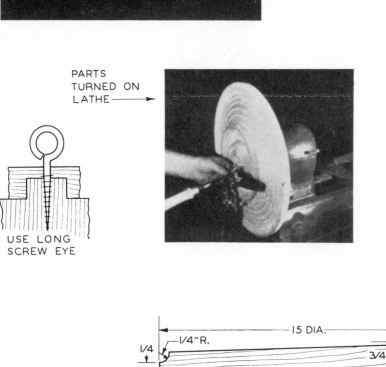

PARTS
TURNED ON
LATHE →

USE LONG
SCREW EYE

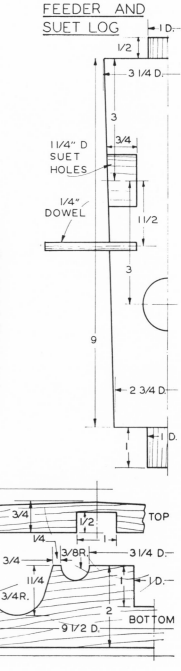

FEEDER AND
SUET LOG

1 D.

1/2

3 1/4 D.

3

3/4

1 1/4" D
SUET
HOLES

1 1/2

1/4"
DOWEL

3

9

2 3/4 D.

1

1 D.

15 DIA.

1/4

1/4" R.

3/4

1/2

TOP

1/4

1

3 1/4 D.

3/8 R.

1 3/8

1/4" GROOVES

3/4

1 3/4

1 1/4

3/4 R.

1 D.

1

2

BOTTOM

DRAIN HOLES

9 1/2 D.

1

18 DIA.

73

platform feeder with suet logs

A platform feeder with suet logs allows you to serve seeds and suet at the same time. The two posts are 3 in. square by 7 in. long. The top is tapered at 45 deg. The two upper, opposite holes in the two posts have rough saw cuts below them to provide a foothold for clinging birds. The other two holes are at the lower end so that the birds can perch on the base of the feeder when eating. The holes are 1¼-in. in diameter; they may be made larger if desired. For the base which is made of ¾-in. stock a solid piece of wood or plywood can be used. Edge strips prevent the loss of seed. In the illustration, screw eyes are used for hanging; however, the eye bolts shown in the illustrations of the log feeders are better.

Give the entire unit a coat of weatherproof stain; do not paint.

bill of materials

Posts:	2–3 x 3	x 7 in.
Base:	1— ¾ x 12	x 24 in.
Side strips:	2— ¾ x	¾ x 24 in.
End strips:	2— ¾ x	¾ x 12 in.
Eye bolts or		
screw eyes:	2— ¼ x 2¼ in.	

platform feeder

This is the simplest feeder you can build. It can be mounted on a wood or metal post. The feeder can be moved about the garden or yard as desired to bring feeding birds closer to a window or to the house. Solid stock or ¾-in. outside plywood can be used. Give the feeder a coat of weatherproof stain but do not use paint.

bill of materials

Base:	1—¾ x 12	x 18 in.
Side strips:	2—¾ x	¾ x 18 in.
End strips:	2—¾ x	¾ x 12 in.

PLATFORM FEEDER
WITH SUET LOGS

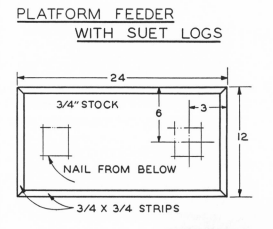

24

3/4" STOCK

6

3

12

NAIL FROM BELOW

3/4 X 3/4 STRIPS

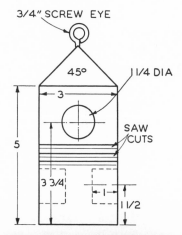

3/4" SCREW EYE

45°

1 1/4 DIA

3

SAW
CUTS

5

3 3/4

1

1 1/2

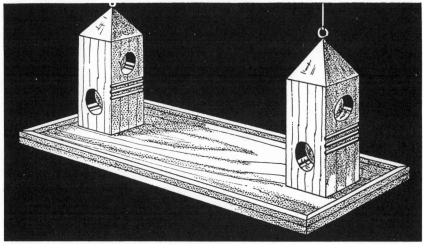

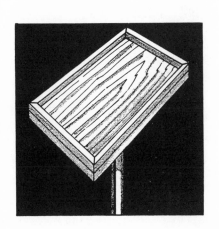

PLATFORM FEEDER

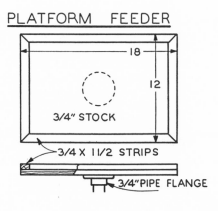

18

12

3/4" STOCK

3/4 X 1 1/2 STRIPS

3/4" PIPE FLANGE

weather-vane feeder

The weather-vane feeder has always been popular because it not only protects the food placed in it; but since it rotates with the wind; it also offers maximum protection to the birds.

Lay out and cut the sides two at a time by nailing the two pieces together. Make all of the other parts. Make the ⅛ by ¼-in. groove in the sidepieces. Note that there are right- and left-hand parts. Make a groove of the same size in the bottom for the glass. Nail cleats to the sidepieces; then attach the bottom with nails. Slide the glass into position and nail on the top. Fit the vanes in place and secure them with two brads. Drill holes for the ¼-in. bolts.

The drawing shows the location of the pivot block. This position was the exact center of gravity of the feeder made by the writer. The center of gravity will be determined by the weight of the stock used. To find the correct position of the hole in the bottom and the location of pivot block on the inside top, balance the completed feeder on some sharp object, such as center point held upside down in a vise. This will accurately locate the center of gravity, and if the feeder is correctly balanced it will swing freely with the wind.

The entire unit can be stained. It can be painted on the outside, but do not paint the floor where the seed is placed.

bill of materials

Sides:	2—	½ x 9 x 9½ in.
Bottom:	1—	½ x 9½ x 15 in.
Front roof:	1—	½ x 3½ x 18 in.
Rear roof:	1—	½ x 9½ x 18 in.
Cleats:	2—	¾ x 1 x 9½ in.
Edge strip:	1—	½ x ¾ x 16 in.
Vanes:	2—	½ x 5 x 22 in.
Pivot block:	1—2	x 2 x 1 in.
Pivot rod:	1—	½ dia. x 20 in.
Glass:	1—5½ x 15½ in.	
Carriage bolts (with nuts and washers):	4—	¼ x 2½ in.

WEATHER-VANE FEEDER

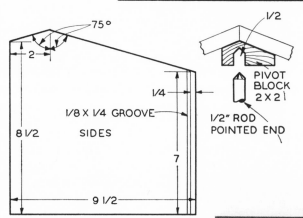

75°

2

1/4

1/8 X 1/4 GROOVE

SIDES

8 1/2

7

9 1/2

1/2

PIVOT
BLOCK
2 X 2

1/2" ROD
POINTED END

ALL STOCK
1/2"

GLASS
5 1/2 X 15 1/2

EDGE STRIPS   1/2 X 3/4 X 16

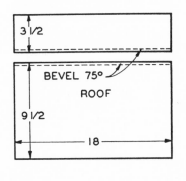

3 1/2

BEVEL 75°

ROOF

9 1/2

18

SIDE
EDGE

NUT
CLEAT
VANE

CORNER CONST.

2

7 1/2

9 1/2

3/4" D.

15

BOT.TOM

1/8 X 1/4
GROOVE

1/4

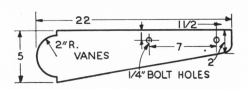

22

1 1/2

2" R.
VANES

5

7

2

1/4" BOLT HOLES

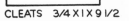

CLEATS   3/4 X 1 X 9 1/2

trolley feeder

The trolley feeder is really a combination feeder in that it has a wire-mesh section on one side to hold suet chunks or suet cakes while the other side has a glass front and is a hopper for seeds. Both sides are protected from the weather by the large, overhanging roof.

Make the end sections first, two at a time, by nailing the pieces together. Cut in grooves as indicated, one for the glass front hopper and the other for the wire mesh. Since right- and left-hand pieces are involved, be careful to locate the grooves correctly. Then cut the other pieces. Nail cross cleats to the sidepieces; then nail the divider in place. Next nail on the bottom from below and then the top centerpiece. Bevel the top sidepieces, put in the wire mesh, and nail this top piece in place. There is enough room above the wire mesh to slip in the suet cakes.

The opposite top piece covering the glass hopper is hinged to facilitate replenishing of the seed. It is a good plan to check the dimensions of the glass to see that it fits in the grooves. Nail on the side bottom edge cleats and then the two ornamental brackets. The feeder is supported by screw eyes. Two small blocks held in place with nails will keep the glass off the bottom and allow the seed to pour out on the floor of the feeder.

Give the feeder a coat of weatherproof stain. Allow it to weather before filling it with food.

bill of materials

Ends:	2— $\frac{1}{2}$ x $5\frac{1}{2}$ x $7\frac{1}{2}$ in.
Bottom:	1— $\frac{1}{2}$ x $9\frac{1}{2}$ x 15 in.
Divider:	1— $\frac{1}{2}$ x $7\frac{1}{2}$ x 10 in.
Top center:	1— $\frac{1}{2}$ x 2 x 15 in.
Top sides:	2— $\frac{1}{2}$ x 4 x 15 in.
End edge cleats:	2— $\frac{1}{2}$ x $\frac{3}{4}$ x $8\frac{1}{2}$ in.
Side edge cleats:	2— $\frac{1}{2}$ x $\frac{3}{4}$ x 14 in.
Brackets:	2— $\frac{1}{2}$ x $1\frac{1}{2}$ x $3\frac{1}{2}$ in.
Hinges (with screws):	2—1 x 1 in.
Screw eyes:	2—$1\frac{1}{2}$ in. long
Glass:	1—$6\frac{1}{2}$ x $10\frac{1}{4}$ in.
Wire mesh:	1—4 x $10\frac{1}{4}$ in.

The illustration below shows how the feeder can be put up as a trolley. A pulley must be installed at both ends of the line. A stout rope or a flexible cable can be used to support the feeder and to pull it back and forth at the same time. The cable or rope is run through both screw eyes, then through a pulley at either end, and finally fastened to the screw eyes on the feeder. This is a good arrangement for winter feeding to bring the feeder closer to the window day by day. It also can be operated from a second-story window where the feeder cannot be reached from the ground for refilling.

TROLLEY FEEDER

GLASS: 6 1/2 X 10 1/4
WIRE MESH: 4 X 10 1/4
ALL STOCK 1/2"

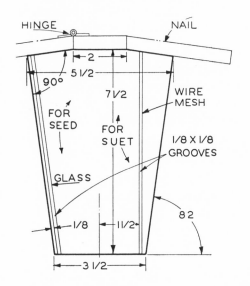

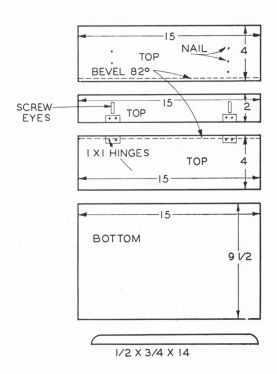

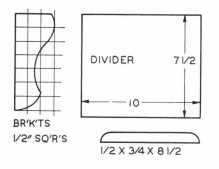

combination feeder

The combination feeder is a smaller version of the trolley feeder shown on the preceding page. It holds loose seed and suet cakes at the same time, one on either side. The food is completely protected from the weather.

Make the end sections first, two at a time, by nailing the pieces together. Cut the grooves as shown in the drawing, one for the glass front hopper and the other for the wire mesh. Since you are dealing with right- and left-hand pieces, cut these grooves with care. Now cut the other pieces. Nail cross cleats to the side pieces; then nail in the divider. Next nail on the bottom from below and then the top centerpiece. Bevel the top side pieces, put in the wire mesh, and nail this top section in place. There is enough room above the wire mesh to slip in the suet cakes.

The opposite top piece covering glass hopper is hinged for refilling with seed. Check the size of the glass to see that it fits in the grooves. Then nail on the side bottom edge cleats and the two ornamental brackets. The feeder is supported by screw eyes. Two small blocks held in place with nails will keep the glass off the bottom and allow the seed to spread out on the floor of the feeder.

Give the feeder a coat of weatherproof stain. Allow it to weather before filling with food.

bill of materials

Ends:	2— ½ x 5½ x 7½ in.
Bottom:	1— ½ x 9½ x 9½ in.
Divider:	1— ½ x 5 x 7½ in.
Top, center:	1— ½ x 2 x 9½ in.
Top, sides:	2— ½ x 4 x 9½ in.
End and sides edge cleats:	4— ½ x ¾ x 8½ in.
Brackets:	2— ½ x 1½ x 3½ in.
Hinges (with screws):	2—1 x 1 in.
Screw eye:	1—1½ in. long
Glass:	1—5¼ x 6½ in.
Wire mesh:	1—5¼ x 4 in.

COMBINATION
FEEDER

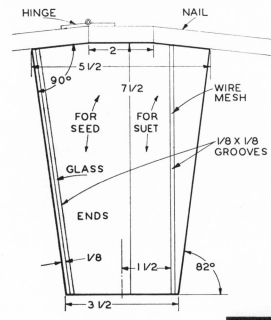

HINGE   NAIL

2

5 1/2

90°

7 1/2

WIRE
MESH

FOR
SEED

FOR
SUET

1/8 X 1/8
GROOVES

GLASS

ENDS

1/8

1 1/2

82°

3 1/2

GLASS: 5 1/4 X 6 1/2
WIRE MESH: 5 1/4 X 4

ALL STOCK
1/2"

BR'K'TS. 1/2" SQ'R'S

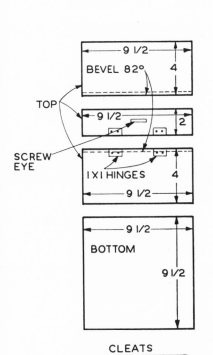

9 1/2

BEVEL 82°   4

9 1/2

2

TOP

SCREW
EYE

I X I HINGES   4

9 1/2

9 1/2

BOTTOM

9 1/2

CLEATS

1/2 X 3/4 X 8 1/2
MAKE FOUR

DIVIDER

7 1/2

5

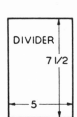

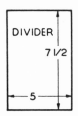

81

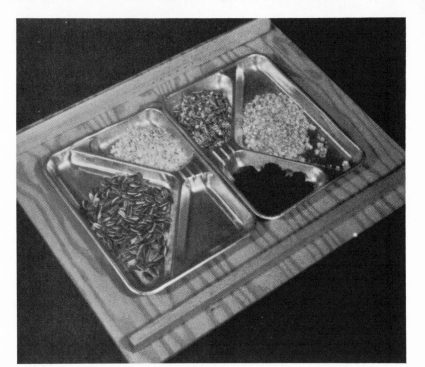

Compartmentalized
Feeding Tray

window-shelf feeder

The window-shelf feeder is very easy to make. It can be attached outside any window and serviced from the inside.

The bottom, or floor, is made from ½-in. stock. Outside plywood will work well. Make the two support brackets out of ¾-in. stock. Bevel the ends so that they fit the slope of the window sill to keep the feeder level. After the dowel perch is inserted, mount the bottom onto the brackets and nail on the sides. Mount the feeder on a sill and hold it in place with wood screws.

This window-shelf feeder is a seed feeder, but to make it more useful you can add a suet feeder as illustrated. Screw the suet feeder to the floor from beneath.

bill of materials

Bottom:	1—	½ x 9 x 15 in.
Brackets:	2—	¾ x 1¼ x 17 in.
Ends:	2—	½ x 2½ x 9 in.
Sides:	2—	½ x 1¼ x 16 in.
Dowels for perch:	1—	½-in. dia. x 14½ in.
Wood screws:	4—	2½ in. long

WINDOW-SHELF FEEDER

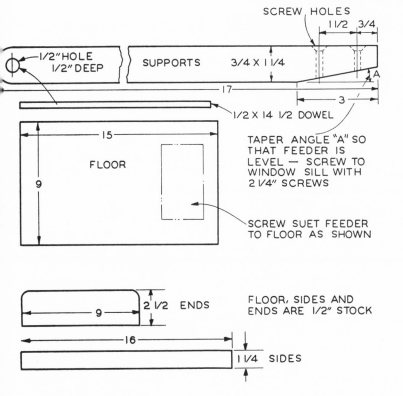

SCREW HOLES

1 1/2   3/4

SUPPORTS   3/4 X 1 1/4

1/2" HOLE
1/2" DEEP

A

17

3

1/2 X 14 1/2 DOWEL

15

FLOOR

9

TAPER ANGLE "A" SO
THAT FEEDER IS
LEVEL — SCREW TO
WINDOW SILL WITH
2 1/4" SCREWS

SCREW SUET FEEDER
TO FLOOR AS SHOWN

9   2 1/2   ENDS

16

1 1/4   SIDES

FLOOR, SIDES AND
ENDS ARE 1/2" STOCK

glass-top window feeder

Glass-top window feeders like the one shown have always been popular and many of them have been made by home-craftsmen and shop students. This feeder gives very good protection to the food placed in it and the birds like to get inside and scratch around.

Make the two end pieces first, nailing them together and cutting them to size at the same time for accuracy. Make the ⅛-in. glass grooves at the top. Since these are cut in right- and left-hand pieces, use care in laying them out. Now cut all the other pieces. Bevel the ends of the supporting brackets to fit the slope of the sill so that the feeder will be level. Insert the dowel perch, nail the bottom to the supports, and then nail on the sides.

The glass edge strips are made from the same piece; that is, one piece is simply reversed or turned upside down to make the second piece. Nail on the edge strips. Slip the glass into the grooves in the side pieces and then nail in the beveled side pieces as indicated.

Screw the feeder to the sill. If the feeder seems to be in need of more support, install an angle bracket below it. Give it a coat of weatherproof stain, but be sure to allow it to weather before putting it into use.

bill of materials

Sides:	2— ½ x 7½ x 8 in.
Bottom:	1— ½ x 9¼ x 15 in.
Support brackets:	2— ¾ x 1 x 17 in.
Glass side strips (beveled and grooved)	2— ¾ x 1¾ x 15 in.
Perch:	1— ½-in. dia. x 14½ in.
Glass:	1—5 x 15½ in.
Wood screws:	4—2½ in. long

GLASS—TOP WINDOW FEEDER

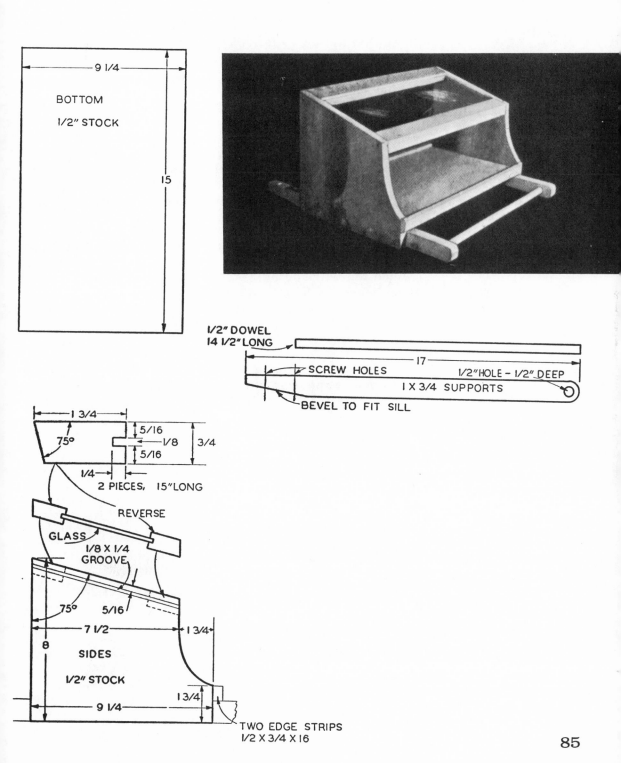

9 1/4

BOTTOM
1/2" STOCK

15

1/2" DOWEL
14 1/2" LONG

17

SCREW HOLES

1/2"HOLE – 1/2" DEEP

1 X 3/4 SUPPORTS

BEVEL TO FIT SILL

1 3/4

75°

5/16
1/8
5/16

3/4

1/4

2 PIECES, 15"LONG

REVERSE

GLASS

1/8 X 1/4
GROOVE

75°   5/16

7 1/2

1 3/4

8

SIDES

1/2" STOCK

9 1/4

1 3/4

TWO EDGE STRIPS
1/2 X 3/4 X 16

85

hopper feeder I

If you put up two or three hopper feeders, they will attract many birds to your yard. They can be mounted on trees and posts, or even on the side of the house or on window frames.

Nail together the stock for the sides, and cut the two pieces at one time. Cut the grooves for the glass front. In making these cuts remember that you are working with right- and left-hand pieces. Cut the other pieces. Nail the back to the bottom, and then nail on the sides. Cut the edge strips and nail them around the edge of the floor to form a retaining wall for the seed.

The next step is to fit the top. Note that a 1 by 1-in. brass hinge is cut in half to form the two hinges. Attach the hinged top with the hinges. Cut two small blocks and nail them below the bottom of the glass. These blocks will keep the glass off the floor of the feeder and allow the seed to pour out easily. A hopper feeder of this design protects the seed at all times.

Give the feeder a coat of weatherproof stain. Allow the finish to weather before the feeder is put up.

bill of materials

Sides:	2—	½ x 3	x	8½ in.
Floor or bottom:	1—	½ x 4	x	5 in.
Back:	1—	½ x 5	x	10¾ in.
Edge strip:	1—	½ x ¾	x	12 in.
Lid at top:	1—	½ x 3¾	x	7 in.
Glass:	1—5¼ x 6¾ in.			
Hinge (with screws):	1—1	x 1		in.

HOPPER FEEDER 1

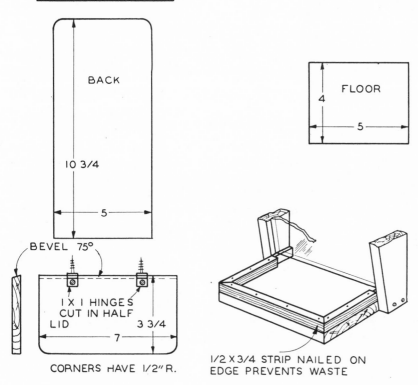

BACK

10 3/4

5

BEVEL 75°

1 X 1 HINGES
CUT IN HALF
LID

7

3 3/4

CORNERS HAVE 1/2" R.

FLOOR

4

5

1/2 X 3/4 STRIP NAILED ON
EDGE PREVENTS WASTE

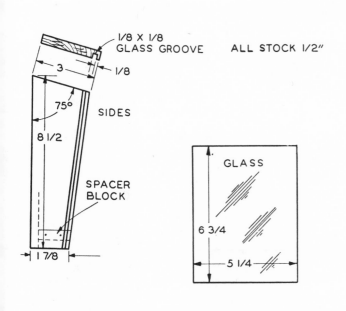

1/8 X 1/8
GLASS GROOVE

ALL STOCK 1/2"

3

1/8

75°

SIDES

8 1/2

SPACER
BLOCK

1 7/8

GLASS

6 3/4

5 1/4

87

suet-seed feeder

This suet-seed feeder is the companion to the hopper feeder shown on the preceding pages. It is also of the hopper type but has a wire-mesh front through which the birds can reach and eat the suet. This versatile feeder can be stocked with chunks of natural suet, pure suet cakes, or suet-seed cakes.

Make the two side pieces first. Nail the stock for them together and cut them at the same time. Cut the grooves for the wire mesh. Be careful in making these grooves because the pieces are right- and left-hand. Then make other pieces. Nail the back to the floor, and then nail on the side pieces with the grooves to the inside. Insert the wire mesh and nail on the top, which is not hinged. The wire can be slid up and down and there is enough space to insert the suet above the wire. Now nail on the edge pieces.

Give the feeder a coat of outside stain and allow it to weather before it is put up.

Milwaukee Public Museum Photo

Four hungry mouths to feed. With a suet-seed feeder nearby, it is easier for this busy parent to take care of its young.

bill of materials

Sides:	2— ½ x 3	x 8½ in.
Floor:	1— ½ x 4	x 5 in.
Back:	1— ½ x 5	x 10¾ in.
Top:	1— ½ x 4	x 7 in.
Edge strips:	1— ¼ x ¾	x 10 in.
Wire mesh:	1—4	x 5¼ in. with ½-in. mesh

SUET – SEED FEEDER

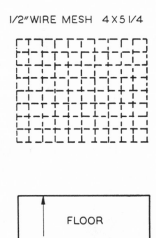

1/2" WIRE MESH 4 X 5 1/4

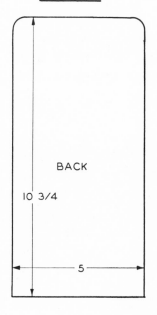

BACK

10 3/4

5

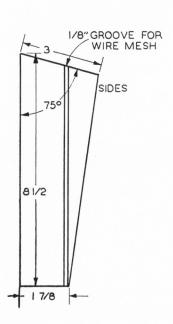

3

1/8" GROOVE FOR WIRE MESH

SIDES

75°

8 1/2

1 7/8

FLOOR

4

5

FLOOR EDGE STRIPS

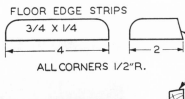

3/4 X 1/4

4

2

ALL CORNERS 1/2"R.

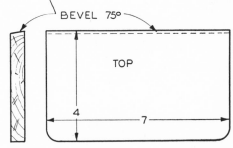

BEVEL 75°

TOP

4

7

ALL STOCK
1/2

89

st. francis feeder

This is an exceptionally attractive garden ornament as well as a practical seed and suet feeder. The figure of St. Francis is 12¾ inches high (without plastic base) and made of plastic. Your local dealer should be able to supply you with one.*

Make the back first and see that all dimensions are accurate. Then nail on the suet rack pieces. Next, nail on the sides and see that the angles correspond with those of the back piece. Fit the statue to a 1⅝-inch base block. You may have to cut a circular piece of ½-inch wood stock to fit inside the base of the statue. Nail this to the base and drill holes in the statue so that it can be fastened to the block with brass screws. Then nail the base to the plywood bottom. Install the side and back assembly and nail it in place. Nail on the roof boards being sure of a tight fit at the ridge. The ridge may be covered with a tin strip. Nail on the edge strips and insert mesh in the suet rack.

Use outside stain to have the feeder match your house or garden furniture as desired.

bill of materials

Sides:	2— ½ x 3½ x 12½ in.
Back:	1— ½ x 12 x 21½ in.
Roof:	2— ½ x 6¼ x 18 in.
Bottom:	1— ¾ x 9½ x 14¼ in.
Suet-rack sides:	2— ¾ x 2 x 5¼ in.
Edge strips:	1— ¼ x 1¼ x 12¾ in.
	2— ¼ x 1¼ x 9 in.
	2— ¼ x 1¼ x 4 in.
Base:	1—1⅝ x 5 x 6½ in.
Suet mesh:	1—5 x 7 in.

* You can also write to Hartland Plastics, Hartland, Wis.

ST. FRANCIS
FEEDER

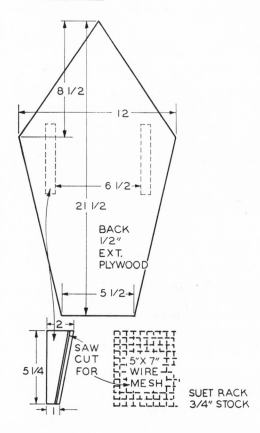

8 1/2

12

6 1/2

21 1/2

BACK
1/2"
EXT.
PLYWOOD

5 1/2

2

SAW
CUT
FOR

5 1/4

1

5" X 7"
WIRE
MESH

SUET RACK
3/4" STOCK

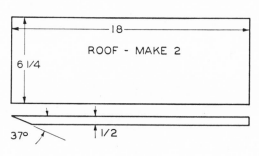

18

ROOF - MAKE 2

6 1/4

37°   1/2

3 1/2

40°

6 1/2

5   BASE

12 1/2   1/2

SIDES

76°   14°

CUT TO FIT
BASE OF
STATUE

1 5/8

12 3/4

1/4" STOCK   BEVEL 14°

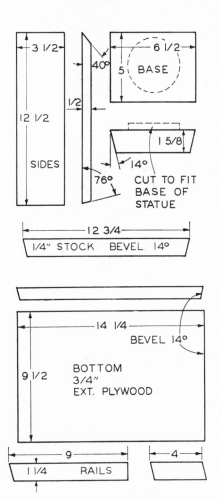

14 1/4

BEVEL 14°

9 1/2

BOTTOM
3/4"
EXT. PLYWOOD

9   4

1 1/4   RAILS

easily built hummingbird feeder

One of the most interesting birds for study is the hummingbird. This sturdy little bird weighs about the same as two sheets of paper and flys, non-stop, across the Gulf of Mexico during migration. The hummingbird is also one of the most attractive visitors to our gardens, and providing a feeder for him is therefore a "must." The feeder is simple to make. Use a small glass or plastic tube about 3 inches long and ⅝ inches in diameter; either a Clinitestube, available at most drugstores, or an ordinary toothbrush holder would do. Wrap a piece of electrician's tape around the end as shown. This provides a "cushion" for the twisted wire that holds the tube to the stake.

To make the unit more attractive and of greater appeal to the hummingbird, you can simulate a flower as shown in the picture to the right (instructions are given in the line drawing). Using very thin aluminum—such as an offset plate or multilith plate easily obtainable from a printer—glue the metal and glass with epoxy cement, and then wrap a piece of tape over the metal as shown. Paint the petals of the "flower" bright red.

The stick for the feeder should be about 3 feet long. Place the feeder right in the middle of your flower bed. For food, use a mixture of two parts water to one part sugar. Fill the feeder with an eye dropper.

¼ cup sugar ½ cup water.
½ "   1 "   For 2 feeders

1 pt sugar 2 pts water.

Do not place in full sun — Dilutes. Wasps.

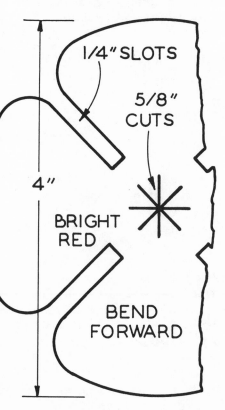

1/4" SLOTS

5/8" CUTS

4"

BRIGHT RED

BEND FORWARD

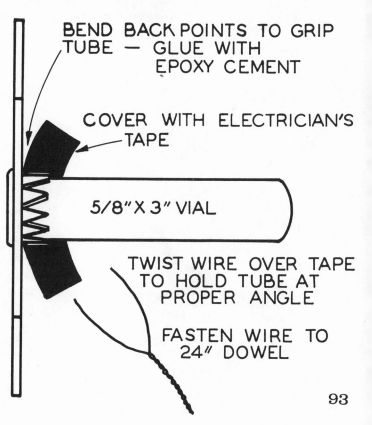

BEND BACK POINTS TO GRIP TUBE — GLUE WITH EPOXY CEMENT

COVER WITH ELECTRICIAN'S TAPE

5/8" X 3" VIAL

TWIST WIRE OVER TAPE TO HOLD TUBE AT PROPER ANGLE

FASTEN WIRE TO 24" DOWEL

93

hopper feeder II

This is a trim, neat feeder that is simple to make and easy to stock with food. Cut an opening in the top for a 3-in. section of tin can, open at the top and bottom. Seal it into the top with putty. Select another tin can that will fit over the can in the top, cut it down to 3 inches, and place it over the can section in the top. This makes a watertight, easy method of filling the hopper with seeds. Be sure that the grooves in the side pieces for the glass panels have the same angles. Carefully follow the dimensions for the seed tray and the opening below the glass panels so that the seed will flow freely without waste. You may have to experiment here a bit.

Make the sides and nail them in place, being certain that the glass panels fit. Then assemble the top with the can opening and drip strips, and screw it in place. Complete the feeder by nailing on the edge strips. Make two seed-fat racks so that one can be filled indoors to replace an empty one on the feeder. Note that the edge strips on all feeders are open at the corners to allow drainage of water.

bill of materials

Sides:	2— ¾ x 9 x 7½ in.
Bottom:	1— ¾ x 27 x 27 in.
Top:	1— ¾ x 9½ x 13 in.
Edge strips:	4— ½ x 1¼ x 25½ in.
Seed racks:	2—1⅝ x 8¾ x 7⅛ in.
Drip strips:	2— ¾ x 1 x 9½ in.
Tray strips:	2— ¼ x 11/16 x 5 in.
Tin cans:	3—3⅞-in. and 4⅛-in dia.
Seed tray, galv.:	1—5 x 7 in.
Glass:	2—8 x 8 in.

Knob, brass screws, wire mesh, L hooks, nails, screw eyes

HOPPER FEEDER II

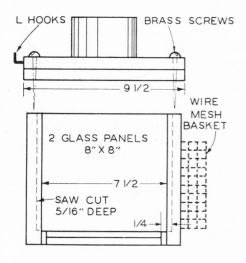

L HOOKS   BRASS SCREWS

9 1/2

WIRE
MESH
BASKET

2 GLASS PANELS
8" X 8"

7 1/2

SAW CUT
5/16" DEEP

1/4

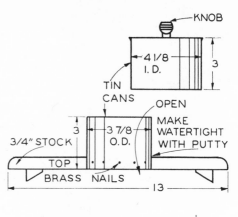

KNOB

4 1/8
I. D.

3

TIN
CANS

OPEN

3   3 7/8
O.D.

MAKE
WATERTIGHT
WITH PUTTY

3/4" STOCK

TOP

BRASS NAILS

13

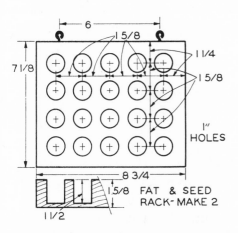

6

1 5/8

7 1/8

1 1/4

1 5/8

1"
HOLES

8 3/4

1 5/8   FAT & SEED
RACK- MAKE 2

1 1/2

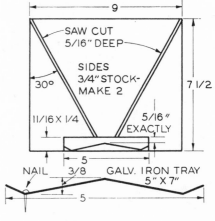

9

SAW CUT
5/16" DEEP

SIDES
3/4" STOCK-
MAKE 2

30°

7 1/2

11/16 X 1/4

5/16"
EXACTLY

NAIL   3/8   GALV. IRON TRAY
5

5" X 7"

5

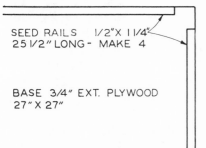

SEED RAILS   1/2"X 1 1/4"
25 1/2" LONG - MAKE 4

BASE 3/4" EXT. PLYWOOD
27" X 27"

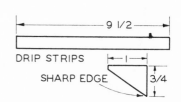

9 1/2

DRIP STRIPS   1

SHARP EDGE   3/4

95

cider-bottle feeder

A cider bottle makes an excellent hopper since the seed is kept dry and free flowing. The bottle rests on a strip that must be exactly 5/16 in. thick—if it is thinner the seed will not flow out; if it is thicker the seed will flow too freely and be wasted. The upright is shown 11 in. high for the ½-gallon bottle used. Check this dimension for your bottle —it should be ¾ in. more than the height of the bottle. The bottle is kept in position by placing or hooking it over a heavy iron peg made from the point of an 8-penny nail. Drill the hole for the nail in the 5/16-in. strip (B) to keep the strip from splitting. The dowels on the underside of the top, which form an enclosure for the bottle, are spaced so there is no binding.

Fill the bottle, place your thumb over the opening, invert the bottle, insert it in the dowel enclosure, and then bring the bottle down and hook it behind the nail peg in the base. Procure two bottles which are exactly alike and make two seed-fat racks. Fill one set indoors to be taken outside to replace the empty set. If you are so equipped, only one trip outside will be required to refill your feeder in cold weather.

bill of materials

Upright:	1— ¾ x 6¾ x 11 in.
Top:	1— ¾ x 6¾ x 10 in.
Base:	1— ¾ x 24 x 24 in.
Cleat (A):	1—1⅝ x 2 x 6¾ in.
Spacer (B):	1—5/16 x ¾ x 3 in.
Dowels:	5— ¼-in. dia. x 2 in.
Edge strips:	2— ½ x ½ x 24 in.
	2— ½ x ½ x 20 in.
Seed racks:	2—1⅝ x 7½ x 7½ in.

½-gal. cider bottle, headless nail, screw eyes, L hooks, nails

BOTTLE FEEDER

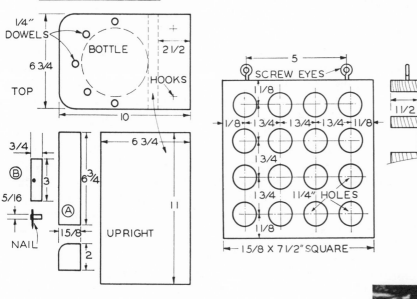

TOP
- 1/4" DOWELS
- BOTTLE
- 6 3/4
- 2 1/2
- HOOKS
- 10

- 3/4
- B
- 3
- 5/16
- NAIL
- A
- 6 3/4
- 15/8
- 2
- UPRIGHT
- 6 3/4
- 11

- 5 — SCREW EYES
- 1 1/8
- 1/8
- 1 3/4
- 1 3/4
- 1 3/4
- 1 1/8
- 1 3/4
- 1 3/4
- 1 1/4" HOLES
- 1 1/8
- 1 1/2
- 15/8 X 7 1/2" SQUARE

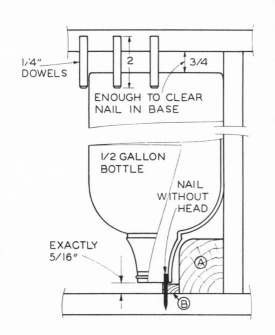

- 1/4" DOWELS
- 2
- 3/4
- ENOUGH TO CLEAR NAIL IN BASE
- 1/2 GALLON BOTTLE
- NAIL WITHOUT HEAD
- EXACTLY 5/16"
- A
- B

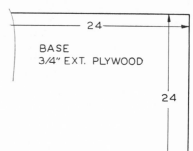

- 24
- BASE 3/4" EXT. PLYWOOD
- 24

- 1/2 X 1/2 EDGE STRIPS MAKE TWO EACH
- 24
- 20

covered feeder

This is the feeder we have outside our breakfast window. One gable end has a replaceable, refillable seed rack; the other gable has a suet basket made of wire mesh. Both rack and seed jar can be filled indoors and easily replaced. A 4½ by 7-inch high peanut-butter jar is used. A 2 by 3-inch hole is cut in the cover. The jar is inverted and, with a 4½-inch diameter stiffener, is bolted to the hopper blocks (B) and formed galvanized-iron seed tray. The horizontal lips of the seed tray slip into grooved sides (A). The 2½ by 7¼-inch seed guard keeps seed from falling out when inverting a jar that has been filled. It is removed when the jar is in place.

Make the roof ends first. Nail on the roof boards and then screw on the uprights. Nail on the slides (A) from below and see that the seed tray slides easily in the grooves. Nail the edge strips to the bottom and screw the bottom to the uprights from below. Make the wire-mesh suet basket and nail it onto one gable. Make two seed-fat racks, one for feeder and the other to keep inside for refilling.

bill of materials

Roof ends:	2— ¾ x 8¼ x 16½ in.
Roof:	1— ½ x 14½ x 28 in.
	1— ½ x 15 x 28 in.
Bottom:	1— ¾ x 17 x 28 in.
Uprights:	4—1⅜-in. dia. x 9 in.
Slides for hopper (A):	2—1 x 1¾ x 8 in.
Edge strips:	2— ½ x 1¼ x 13 in.
	2— ½ x 1¼ x 24 in.
Seed racks:	2—1⅝ x 7½ x 15 in.
Perches:	12— ¼-in. dia. x 4 in.
Dowel:	1— ¼-in. dia. x 3 in.
Seed tray, galv.:	1—9¼ x 7¾ in.
Stiffener:	1—4½-in. dia. to fit cover
Hopper blocks (B):	2—1¼ x 1½ x 5¼ in.
Seed-guard insert:	1—2½ x 7¼ in.
Jar (peanut butter):	1—4½-in. dia. x 7 in. high

COVERED FEEDER

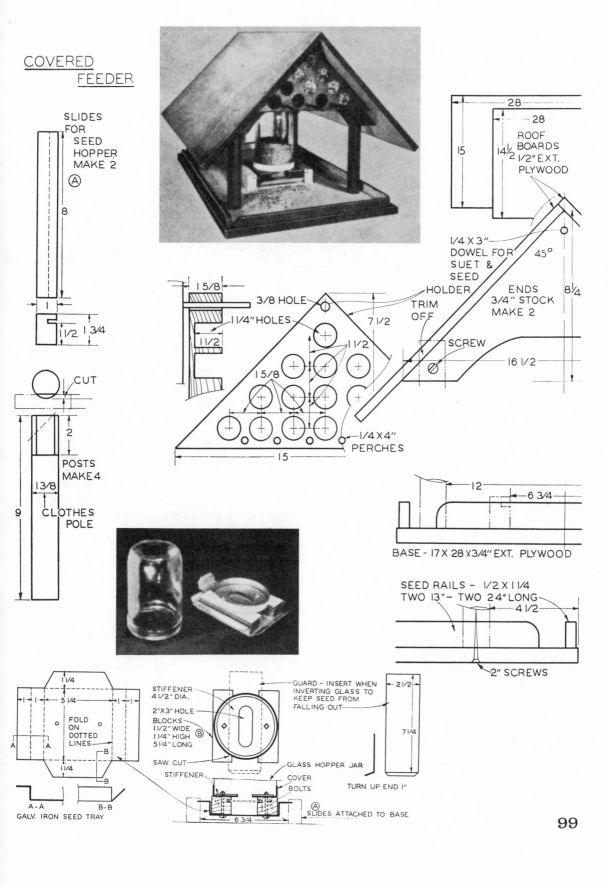

SLIDES FOR SEED HOPPER MAKE 2 (A)

8

1

1 1/2   1 3/4

CUT

2

POSTS MAKE 4

13/8

CLOTHES POLE

9

1 5/8

1 1/2

1 1/4" HOLES

3/8 HOLE

1 1/2

1 5/8

TRIM OFF

7 1/2

1/4 X 3" DOWEL FOR SUET & SEED HOLDER

SCREW

1/4 X 4" PERCHES

15

28

28

15

14 1/2

ROOF BOARDS 1/2" EXT. PLYWOOD

45°

ENDS 3/4" STOCK MAKE 2

8 1/4

16 1/2

12

6 3/4

BASE - 17 X 28 X 3/4" EXT. PLYWOOD

SEED RAILS - 1/2 X 1 1/4
TWO 13" - TWO 24" LONG

4 1/2

2" SCREWS

1 1/4

5 1/4

1 1/4

FOLD ON DOTTED LINES

A   A

B
B

A-A   B-B

GALV. IRON SEED TRAY

STIFFENER 4 1/2" DIA.

2"X 3" HOLE

BLOCKS 1 1/2" WIDE 1 1/4" HIGH 5 1/4" LONG (B)

SAW CUT

STIFFENER

GUARD - INSERT WHEN INVERTING GLASS TO KEEP SEED FROM FALLING OUT

GLASS HOPPER JAR

COVER BOLTS

2 1/2

7 1/4

TURN UP END 1"

(A) SLIDES ATTACHED TO BASE

6 3/4

99

feeder with mason-jar hopper

Here is something new in feeders. It is simple to build and although the feeder has an elaborate appearance, no unusual materials are required. Basically this feeder consists of an inverted Mason jar with holes in the cover which allow the seed to pour out on the triangular platform.

First make the floor or platform out of ¾-in. stock. Outside plywood is very good for this part. Make the rounded end blocks and nail them in place. Then make the side strips and fit them in place. The entire outside can be rounded on a sander if available to make the pieces line up. Next nail the 1 by 1-in. spacer block in place and then drill a ¼-in. hole through it from top to bottom and through the bottom. Screw the screw eyes into each corner block and attach the three chains.

Use a standard pint Mason jar for the hopper. Remove the cover and break out the glass liner. Drill a ¼-in. hole in the exact center of the cover and then drill three ⅞-in. holes as indicated in the drawing. These holes allow the seed to pour out onto the floor. Now cut off the head of a standard ¼-in. dia. by 2-in. bolt. Insert the threaded end of the bolt through the center hole and secure with nuts above and below the cover as shown. Fill the Mason jar with seed, screw on the cover, and insert the bolt end in the hole in the spacer. The feeder is now ready for use.

Give the feeder a coat of outside stain and allow it to weather before putting it up.

bill of materials

Bottom:	1—	¾ x 12 x 13½ in.
Corner blocks:	3—	¾ x 1⅛ x 3⅝ in.
Side strips:	3—	½ x ¾ x 10¾ in.
Spacer block:	1—	1 x 1 x 1 in.
Screw eyes:	3—	1¼ in. long
Furnace chains:	3—16	in. long
Mason jar:	1—	1-pint size
Bolt with nuts:	1—	¼ x 2 in.

FEEDER WITH
GLASS HOPPER

PINT
MASON JAR

COVER

NUTS

1/4 X 2 BOLT
CUT OFF HEAD

HOLES FOR
SEED
7/8" DIA

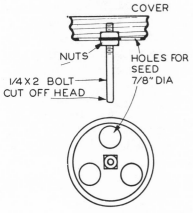

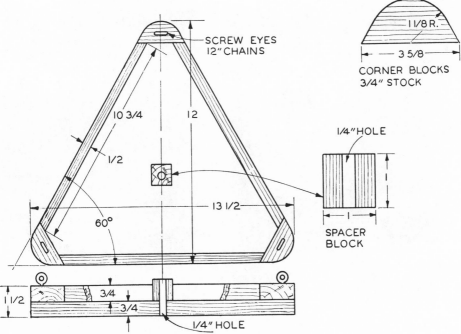

SCREW EYES
12" CHAINS

10 3/4

12

1/2

13 1/2

60°

1 1/2

3/4

3/4

1/4" HOLE

1 1/8 R.

3 5/8

CORNER BLOCKS
3/4" STOCK

1/4" HOLE

1

SPACER
BLOCK

coconut shells as feeders

Coconut shells may be used to make very effective feeders. The feeder shown on the left is made from the hollowed-out shell. Drill a 1⅛- or 1¼-in. hole in the side of the coconut. Score the coconut meat with a knife and break it out using a screw driver. Drill drainage holes at the bottom and a hole at the top for the supporting chain.

The photo on the right shows a coconut cut in half with three small holes drilled around the edge to which the chains are attached. Drainage holes in the bottom prevent rain water from collecting. If desired, two or more of these half shells can be hung one below the other by means of wires. The single shell is best, because when several are hung in tandem, the rain water drains off from one into the other. Such feeders, of course, are protected if they are put up on a porch or under some protective overhang.

There are many other devices that can be made out of old dishes, small wooden bowls, cut-down herring pails, small boxes, and the like. There are countless discarded items that will prove very serviceable as feeders. Why not try to develop one that will have your own originality as its trademark?

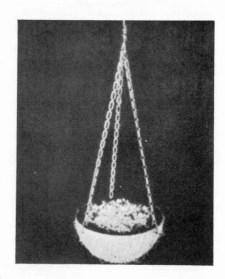

Passenger Pigeon _male & femal_
Columba migratoria

water: the second requirement

The food supply of birds must be complemented by an abundant supply of fresh water. Birds need water for drinking and bathing. Since they use the same water for both purposes, separate containers are not necessary.

In the natural surroundings of birds, water is supplied by brooks, ponds, rain puddles, swamps, dew, and snow. Thus they have more than enough sources of water. But in the average city or suburban lot there are not enough sources of water. To attract and keep birds, an ample supply must be provided.

If you live in the country and have enough room for a bird sanctuary, a watering place for birds can be very easily provided by simply hollowing out a small dish-shaped area in the ground and filling it with water. This unit can become a part of the landscaping by lining the depression with cement and making a small ornamental pool. Do not make the pool too deep. Birds rarely will use a pool or a birdbath that is more than 2 or 3 inches deep. Have the sides at a very flat slope so that entry is easy. The birds will approach the pool more freely if there are no nearby bushes that could hide enemies. Have at least 3 to 4 feet of open space around the pool. Use grass in this area or, better, fine sand and dust for a natural dust bath. These pools can vary in size from 3 to 10 feet across, depending upon the space you can devote to them. The chief objections to this kind of pool are that it occupies too much space in the average yard and is very difficult to clean.

If you are fortunate enough to have a small stream or a running spring on your land, the pool described above can be made a part of it. Widen a section of the stream, give the sides a very gradual slope, provide the grass or dust area, remove close bushes and shrubs, and you will have an excellent, natural bird-watering place.

While bushes should be removed from the area immediately surrounding the pool, have a fence, open bush, dead tree, or overhanging branches about 10 feet away to serve as a place for the birds to rest and preen themselves. Locate the pool and preening perch where they will get both sunshine and shade and the birds will use them constantly.

A shallow pool with sloping sides and lined with concrete is welcomed by the birds.

Leafie Watt—From the National Audubon Society

A dead tree near a bird bath provides an excellent preening place for birds.

the birdbath

Perhaps the common birdbath is the most practical means of providing water for birds. Baths made of terra cotta can be purchased at very reasonable prices. Those made of concrete are more expensive but last longer and are more durable. Regardless of the material of which the birdbath is made, be sure that it is designed correctly. Many of the birdbaths available are too deep and the sides are too steep. The baths should not be more than 3 inches deep and the sides should slope down gradually. The surface of the bowl and edge should be rough to provide a good footing.

On the following pages are instructions for casting a concrete birdbath by the sweep method. The pedestal is of poured concrete. The construction is simple and will be a very interesting experience if you have not worked with concrete before. Once the forms have been made, it is a simple matter to make additional birdbaths. The bowl can be placed on the concrete pedestal or it can be set on a stump if there happens to be one in a good location. You can also place it on a brick pedestal or any suitable mount.

Like pools, birdbaths should be carefully located in an open space with a fence or branches about 10 feet away.

how to make a concrete birdbath

A simple and inexpensive way to make a concrete birdbath is shown here. The bowl is formed with sweeps that mold the core and the concrete to shape. Select a level, flat surface on which to mount a piece of tarred building paper about 36 inches square. Tack it in place at the edges. Drill a hole at the exact center for the ¼-inch pivot, which may be a wood dowel or iron rod and insert the pivot.

Cut the sweep for the core out of 1⅛-inch stock as shown. The bowl is cast or swept upside down. The core is made of clay. To use less clay, you can build up the core out of waste lumber as illustrated. Over this core spread the clay, which should be soft enough to shape easily. Place the sweep on the pivot and work it back and forth until the core is shaped. Allow the core to dry partially and coat it with grease or oil.

When the clay has set, mix the concrete, one part cement to three parts sand and gravel. Keep it rather thick so that it can be formed.

Add the second spacer block, put the concrete over the clay mold, and sweep it into shape. Small pieces of chicken wire can be added as reinforcement. When shaped, trowel the concrete smooth and allow it to harden. After the concrete has set, remove it from the board, and take out the clay core. Round the edges with a brick; then take out the wood spacer block in the center and plug the hole with cement.

Maintenance of the birdbath is an interesting home chore for the youngsters.

108

CONCRETE
BIRD BATH

MADE WITH SWEEPS

1 PART CEMENT
3 PARTS SAND

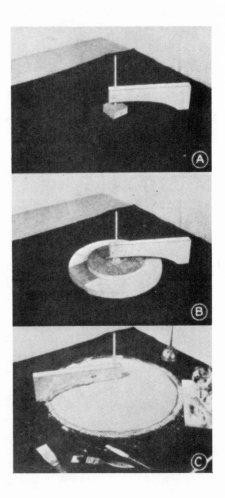

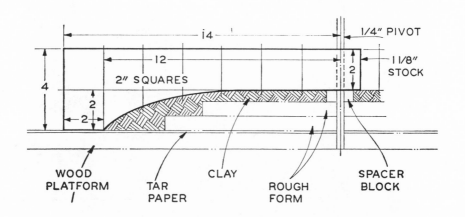

WOOD PLATFORM   TAR PAPER   CLAY   ROUGH FORM   SPACER BLOCK

14

12

2" SQUARES

4

2

2

1/4" PIVOT

1 1/8" STOCK

2

109

FORM OF SWEEP FOR CLAY MOLD

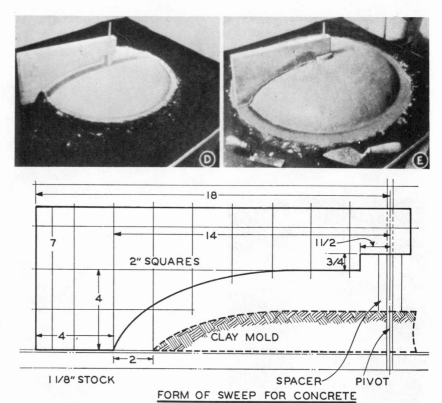

18

14

7

2" SQUARES

1 1/2

3/4

4

4

CLAY MOLD

2

SPACER   PIVOT

1 1/8" STOCK

FORM OF SWEEP FOR CONCRETE

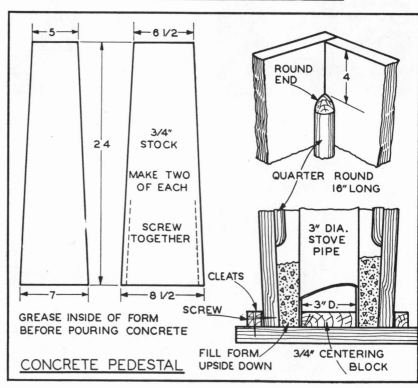

5

6 1/2

ROUND
END

4

24

3/4"
STOCK

MAKE TWO
OF EACH

SCREW
TOGETHER

QUARTER ROUND
16" LONG

3" DIA.
STOVE
PIPE

CLEATS

7

8 1/2

SCREW

3" D.

GREASE INSIDE OF FORM
BEFORE POURING CONCRETE

FILL FORM
UPSIDE DOWN

3/4" CENTERING
BLOCK

CONCRETE PEDESTAL

110

The pedestal is made upside down and is cast. Make the box form as shown on the drawing. To form the hollow center, a 3-inch diameter stovepipe is used as a core. Mount the 3-inch round centering block, put the pipe over it, and then locate the box form around this assembly. One-inch quarter rounds with rounded ends are nailed inside the box to form the corner cove of the finished pedestal. Oil or grease the inside of the mold and pipe. Screw cleats around the form to hold it in place. Then pour the concrete using a rod to eliminate air bubbles.

Color can be added to the concrete if desired. Your local dealer will tell you how much is required to obtain the color you like. The lug on the bottom of the bowl will hold the bowl to the top of the pedestal.

other ways of providing water

A convenient water supply attracts birds old and young.

Milwaukee Public Museum Photo

There are many other ways of providing a birdbath. They are not all as elaborate as those just described. For example, you can use large earthenware pie plates or an ordinary flowerpot setter. The sides of the latter are a bit steep but it will serve the purpose. Any shallow dish or receptacle will do.

The trickle and splash of falling water is an attraction for birds.

Birdbaths can be very elaborate, approximating the formal jet fountains in public parks. Many of these are more decorative than practical. However, a fountain with a jet of water has an attraction for birds. They are fascinated by the trickle and splash of water as you will discover if you provide a fountain in your birdbath, pool, or fountain. Most of the formal birdbaths have permanent water connections and the water must be turned off during freezing weather. The drains, too, must be looked after.

care of birdbaths

Whether a birdbath is simple or elaborate, it must be kept clean. Flush it out every other day and fill it with clean water. You will thus prevent the formation of algae, which not only makes the water unfit for use but also causes an odor. The formation of algae in larger pools and baths can also be prevented by adding one ounce of copper sulfate to every 50 gallons of water. No harmful effects to birds from this solution have ever been noted. Scrub the bowl with a wire brush or with sand and a piece of burlap at least once a week.

winter care

Unless there has been a very dry spell and there is no snow or ice on the ground, it is not necessary to provide water for the birds during the winter. Since birds do not bathe in freezing temperatures, they require water only for drinking and only a very small amount. If a birdbath is maintained during the winter months, the water must be kept from freezing or the bowl will crack. The simplest way to prevent this is to empty the water each day before it has a chance to freeze solid. A birdbath with an electric heater element in it will also keep the water from freezing. Some resourceful craftsmen devise their own heated birdbaths using the element from a discarded toaster. Other bird fanciers place an electric-light bulb in the pedestal base which, when lit, throws off just enough heat to keep the water from freezing. Experimenting with ways of heating birdbaths may prove interesting to you.

the bird dust bath

In addition to water baths, birds also need dust baths. Dust baths rid birds of skin parasites, not lice, as is commonly believed. Fine dust acts also like talcum powder to condition their feathers.

Any shallow tray or box can be used for a dust bath. A box 2 feet wide, 3 feet long, and 2 inches deep is very practical for this purpose. Fill it with ordinary dry dust—road dust is best—and keep the dust dry. Place the dust bath near the birdbath in the sun and one bird after another will make use of it. Ordinary powdered yellow sulphur can be used as a parasiticide. Add one part sulphur to ten parts of dust.

shelter: the third requirement

Your bird-attraction project will be complete when you provide shelter and nesting facilities. Most people regard shelter as the most important requirement; as a matter of fact, food and water are more effective means of attracting birds. But shelter and nesting facilities must be provided, because birds will not stay unless they have a place to build their nests and raise their young.

We have explained how the spreading out of cities over the countryside, deforestation, and the drainage of swamps have curtailed the natural supply of food for birds. These same factors have reduced the shelter available to them. Their cover has been further shrunk by our "clean" pastures and forests with the old dead trees cut down, brush destroyed, and growth along fences removed. Any man-made devices that will help to replace the birds' dwindling supply of natural shelter will be a distinct benefit to them.

Successful bird attraction requires an adequate number of the right kind of birdhouses. Birdhouses must be built for specific types of birds, not just for birds in general, and they must be correctly located and maintained. The construction of birdhouses offers a dual pleasure: first, the enjoyment of making them; second, the adventure of attracting and sheltering birds with them.

know the birds you want to attract

It is common knowledge that wrens will build a nest in almost any type of shelter—an old tin can, a shoe, or a flowerpot. This fact has led many people to believe that all birds are no more selective in their choice of a shelter. This impression is far from the truth. Birds as a rule are very particular about where their nests are built and how they are made. For this reason you must plan a house for a specific bird, making sure that it is the correct size, has the proper opening, and is placed at a predetermined height above the ground. The birdhouses described in this book follow these specifications, and in building them you can be assured that they meet the needs of the birds for which they are intended.

two types of birds

The birds that the amateur bird fancier will want to attract to his birdhouse can be divided into two groups: the tree dwellers and the cavity dwellers. Tree dwellers will not live in a house or any kind of cavity. For example, the Baltimore Oriole will never build a nest in a man-made or a nature-made box. The oriole always builds its own graceful nest out of hair and other weaving materials, suspending it from branches, such as those of the elm tree. On the other hand, woodpeckers always build their nests in the hollow of trees or in other cavities.

A report of the United States Fish and Wildlife Service states that there are more than 50 species of birds that will occupy man-made houses. There should be little difficulty, therefore, in attracting birds to one's premises with good shelters. The tree dwellers, those that build their own nests, can also be encouraged to set up housekeeping on your property. With the right kind of planting, which is discussed on page 41, and with ample food and water supplies, you can also have these birds as your guests during the summer. By pruning trees to provide natural crotches for the nests, by planting the right kind of ground cover, and by supplying materials for nest building, you can encourage them to stay.

nesting materials

In a yard that is kept "spic and span," the birds will not be able to find the natural materials they need to build their nests. No matter how many houses are erected on a lot, no matter how good the trees are for nests, if the birds do not have the grass, string, straw, and other nesting materials, they cannot and will not build. An ample supply must be on hand from which the birds can select the materials they need. String, cotton, wool, and yarn are excellent building materials. See to it, however, that none of the pieces are over 4 inches in length. Birds may become entangled in long pieces and die. In addition to string and yarn, the following should be available:

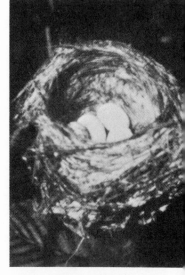

You can attract birds to your home grounds by supplying the proper nesting materials and the proper places for them to build.

Feathers	Down	Moss
Horsehair	Straw	Kapok
(from old upholstery)	Fur	Thread
Bark	Raveled rope	
Excelsior	Cellophane cigar wrappers	
Soft cloth strips		

You will think of other things that birds can use in the construction of their nests. Have some mud on hand for the robins, because, as you know, they line the nest with it.

Have your nesting material available for the birds early in spring, even if there is snow on the ground. The time of the arrival of the first robin is not too soon. If you want, you can build the simple nesting materials box shown on the following pages. With this box, the materials are readily available, are always dry, and the birds can select what they need. An added advantage of this box is that it can be used as a suet feeder after the nesting season.

Milwaukee Public Museum Photos

117

nesting materials box

Very early in spring, perhaps right after the snow leaves, it is a good time to provide nesting materials for the birds. Here is a neat, handy box that stores the materials in one place, keeps them dry and ready for the birds to use, and when the nesting season is over, the box can be used as a suet feeder.

The construction of this neat, handy box is simple. Nail together the stock for the two sides so that these two pieces can be cut in one operation. Drill the ¼-inch holes for the dowels, making one right-hand and one left-hand. Cut all the other pieces. Nail the back to the bottom, and then nail on the sides after the dowels are inserted. Put brads through the dowels. Then fit the top or lid and attach it with a 1 by 1 inch hinge cut in half.

Give the box a coat of weatherproof stain or paint if you want to.

bill of materials

Sides:	2—½ x 3½ x 9¾ in.
Bottom:	1—½ x 6 x 9 in.
Back:	1—½ x 9 x 12 in.
Top:	1—½ x 5 x 12 in.
Dowels:	5—¼-in. dia. x 9¼ in. long
Hinge (with screws):	1—1 x 1 in.

NESTING MATERIALS BOX

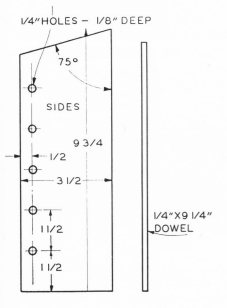

1/4" HOLES — 1/8" DEEP

75°

SIDES

9 3/4

1/2

3 1/2

1 1/2

1 1/2

1/4" X 9 1/4" DOWEL

ALL CORNERS HAVE 1/2" R.

BACK

12

9

ALL STOCK 1/2"

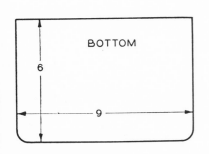

BOTTOM

6

9

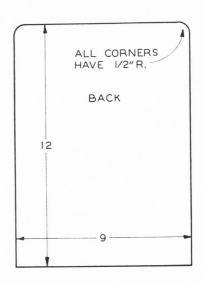

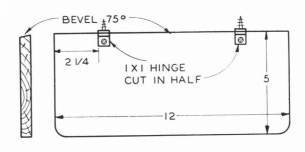

BEVEL 75°

2 1/4

1 X 1 HINGE CUT IN HALF

5

12

commercial birdhouses

Some excellent birdhouses made by reputable firms are on the market. You will find the manufacturers listed in the better periodicals, such as the Audubon Magazine. While they will certainly meet the needs of the bird fancier, the manual training student and homecrafter can make houses that are just as good and cost a lot less. The houses shown on the following pages can be made by anyone. Other birdhouses are also sold that simply do not come up to basic requirements. Painted in bright colors to catch the customer's eye, they frequently are found on the shelves of roadside stands and novelty shops. As a rule they are not the right dimensions, have the wrong-size openings, are made of poor materials, and are constructed unsatisfactorily. They are designed for decoration rather than for bird attraction. This word of warning should be enough to steer you clear of them.

some practical building hints

Here are some suggestions for making any type of birdhouses. First, design it for the bird it is to shelter. Try to duplicate as closely as possible the natural shelter of the bird. A woodpecker, for example, will be more at home in a house covered with bark than one painted green. Second, construct your birdhouses with care, taking special pains to produce accurate, good fitting joints. Third, make the house pleasing in appearance but do not make a garden ornament out of it. You may like fancy designs and bright colors, but birds don't.

The houses on the following pages incorporate almost all of the following suggestions. There will be some variations in the specifications for a particular birdhouse, such as the use of tin or of roofing paper for covering the roof joint. Such variations can be supplied to any of the designs. Use your own imagination to make changes as long as you do not depart from the basic specifications and size. In most instances, the houses may be altered to accommodate other birds by changing the size of the opening and making the house deeper or shallower according to specifications for the species.

The full-page drawing gives the design and construction details for the birdhouse. Here are some suggestions:

1. Build the house for a specific species of bird. This point is so vital that we do not hesitate to repeat it. Each species will require some slight variation which should not be overlooked. Study the specifications carefully and do not alter the basic dimensions.

2. Use the right materials. Wood is the best all-around material for constructing birdhouses. It is a good insulator, it is inexpensive, it is easy to cut and assemble, and it is readily available. Use a softwood, like white pine. Pine is easy to work and can be bought at any lumberyard. Cedar is good also. Cypress will never rot but it is difficult to get, hard to drive nails into, and expensive. All of the houses in this book are made of ½-inch stock unless otherwise indicated. Pine of this thickness is simple to work, but if you cannot get it, use ¾-inch stock. In this event you may have to vary a few of the dimensions. Another excellent material is ½-inch outside plywood. It is more expensive, but the big sheets allow you to plan and cut your wood with a minimum of waste.

For the rustic type of house use air-dried logs. These may have checks in them, but when they are hollowed out, the imperfections do not matter. For roofs use slab stock with the bark on it if available. If possible, avoid using metal. It is too hot in summer and provides a poor foothold for both young and old birds.

3. It is not necessary to have a landing perch on smaller houses. A perch makes it simple for sparrows and other bothersome birds to enter nests where they are not wanted. Often the perch is added just for appearance.

4. Assemble securely. Use copper or aluminum nails to assemble birdhouses. Better still, use brass screws. Ordinary nails should be avoided because they soon rust and the house will fall apart.

5. Leave the inside rough. If you are going to use ½-inch lumber, your lumberman will take heavier stock and split it. He may want to smooth the lumber by running it through the planer but ask that it be left rough. When you build the house, lay out the pieces so that the rough surface will be on the inside when the house is assembled. The rough wood gives the baby birds, and the old ones as well, something to hang onto when crawling out of the nest. Some

books advise that the rough surfaces be located on the outside for rustic appearance. This suggestion is well intended but impractical. Lumber that is rough on both sides will provide both a foothold for the birds on the inside and a rustic appearance on the outside.

6. Provide ventilation. If a small house, poorly ventilated, is located in the sun and occupied by four or five baby birds, it can become so hot they will suffocate. You can provide adequate circulation by having vent holes at the top of the house below the extended roof boards. In some cases the sidepieces can be cut an eighth of an inch short so that there will be a vent along the upper side of the house.

7. Be sure that the house drains. If the bottom of the house is "glove-tight," any rain that seeps in or is driven in during a storm may accumulate and cause baby birds to drown. Drain holes in the bottom will prevent the house from flooding. All the houses in this book have swing-out bottoms for easy cleaning and are loosely fitted so that moisture cannot collect.

8. Have a tight roof. Generally, when the boards have been accurately cut and fitted, the roof will be waterproof. As an added precaution you can nail a tin strip over the ridge or cover it with roofing paper.

9. Protect the opening. See to it that the roof boards extend well over the front or opening side of the house. This overhang prevents rain from being blown into the house.

10. Be sure the house is easy to clean. In the houses shown there is a pivot screw at each side of the bottom toward the rear. Another screw holds the bottom at the front of the house. When the front screw is removed, the bottom swings out so that the entire inside may be cleaned. This is a simple way to make a house easy to clean without the use of hinges and other unnecessary hardware. The houses should be cleaned each year, late in fall or very early spring, to remove the old nest and any bugs or debris from the previous season. Do not wash out the house with soap and water unless you are positive that lice are present. If you like, you can put a very little, clean, new excelsior in the bottom of the house as a welcome for the new birds.

11. Give the house a suitable finish. Birdhouses can be painted and stained. A finish that will protect them against the weather may be preferred. However, select colors that are dull and drab; do not look for the brightest orange,

GENERAL CONSTRUCTION IDEAS

EQUAL BEVEL ROOF BOARDS

KEEP AT CONVENIENT ANGLE SUCH AS 60°

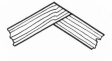

OVERLAPPING ROOF BOARDS

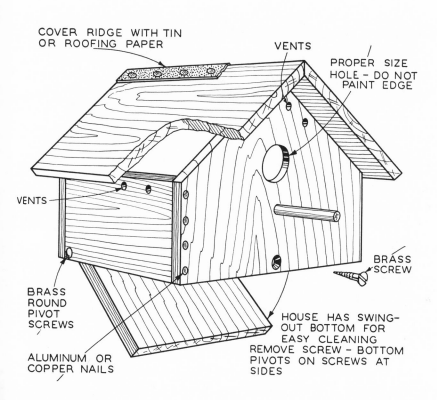

COVER RIDGE WITH TIN OR ROOFING PAPER

VENTS

PROPER SIZE HOLE – DO NOT PAINT EDGE

VENTS

BRASS ROUND PIVOT SCREWS

ALUMINUM OR COPPER NAILS

BRASS SCREW

HOUSE HAS SWING-OUT BOTTOM FOR EASY CLEANING REMOVE SCREW – BOTTOM PIVOTS ON SCREWS AT SIDES

USE 1/2" OR 3/4" STOCK

ROUGH LUMBER IS BEST

DO NOT PAINT OR STAIN INSIDE OF HOUSE

ROOF SHOULD PROTECT ENTRANCE

PERCH MAY OR MAY NOT BE ADDED AS DESIRED

MOUNT HOUSE IN MOST CONVENIENT WAY – HANGING, ON POST OR ON SIDE OF BUILDING OR TREE

MOUNT AT PROPER HEIGHT

Dimensions of Birdhouses and Height They Should Be Placed Above the Ground

Bird	Inside of House	Depth of House	Size of Entrance	Entrance Above Floor	Height Above Ground
	Dimensions in Inches				Feet
Bewick's Wren	4 x 4	6 to 8	1	1 to 6	6 to 10
Carolina Wren	4 x 4	6 to 8	1⅛	1 to 6	6 to 10
Chickadee	4 x 4	8 to 10	1⅛	6 to 8	6 to 15
Downy Woodpecker	4 x 4	8 to 10	1¼	6 to 8	6 to 20
House Wren	4 x 4	6 to 8	1	1 to 6	6 to 10
Nuthatch	4 x 4	8 to 10	1¼	6 to 8	12 to 20
Titmouse	4 x 4	8 to 10	1¼	6 to 8	6 to 15
Bluebird	5 x 5	8	1½	6	5 to 10
Tree Swallow	5 x 5	6	1½	1 to 5	10 to 15
Violet-Green Swallow	5 x 5	6	1½	1 to 5	10 to 15
Crested Flycatcher	6 x 6	8 to 10	2	6 to 8	8 to 20
Golden-Fronted Woodpecker	6 x 6	12 to 15	2	9 to 12	12 to 20
Hairy Woodpecker	6 x 6	12 to 15	1½	9 to 12	12 to 20
House Finch	6 x 6	6	2	4	8 to 12
Purple Martin	6 x 6	6	2½	1	15 to 20
Redheaded Woodpecker	6 x 6	12 to 15	2	9 to 12	12 to 20
Saw-Whet Owl	6 x 6	10 to 12	2½	8 to 10	12 to 20
Starling	6 x 6	16 to 18	2	14 to 16	10 to 25
Flicker	7 x 7	16 to 18	2½	14 to 16	6 to 20
Screech Owl	8 x 8	12 to 15	3	9 to 12	10 to 30
Sparrow Hawk	8 x 8	12 to 15	3	9 to 12	10 to 30
Barn Owl	10 x 18	15 to 18	6	4	12 to 18
Wood Duck	10½ x 10½	24	3	20	10 to 25
SHELF NESTS					
Barn Swallow	6 x 6	6	(A)		8 to 12
Phoebe	6 x 6	6	(A)		8 to 12
Robin	6 x 8	8	(A)		6 to 15
Song Sparrow	6 x 6	6	(B)		1 to 3

(A) One or more sides open
(B) All sides open

red, or blue and expect the birds to flock to a house so decorated. Bright colors frighten birds and they will not come near them. Repainted old houses or new ones, if put up in the fall, will have the entire winter to weather and lose their "new look." Never paint or stain the inside of the house and do not paint or stain within ¼ inch of the opening. The feel of unfinished wood is more natural to birds than that of a painted surface. An exception to the principle of applying drab finishes on birdhouses is the use of white on martin houses. The light-reflecting qualities of white keep the house cooler and seem to attract this species.

12. Use tested mounting and hanging arrangements. Shown on page 128 are several methods for hanging or supporting houses. Do not use ordinary screw eyes for hanging a house. They will hold when the house is new but after a short time the screws loosen up, water seeps into the holes, and the screw eyes pull out. If this occurs the house will fall and any young within will die or be injured.

construction: tools and procedures

The houses have been designed to accommodate the skill of the beginner and the average home craftsman, not the experienced carpenter, and so the construction is simple. The ordinary woodworking tools such as saw, square, and hammer, and other simple tools are all you will need. Of course, power tools such as a jig saw, band saw, drill press, and circular saw make possible faster construction and very accurate work.

lumber

Lumber is expensive so it is worth your while to find a place where you can get it at a low cost or where you can obtain used wood. Discarded boxes have always made good birdhouse material. Apple boxes, pear boxes, and, as a matter of fact, all fruit boxes are excellent. Crating from furniture stores, boxes that are used to ship printing paper, and countless other types of shipping crates are made of very usable lumber. Often this is scrapped and you can have it if you haul it away. The wood is dry and seasoned.

Do not try to take boxes apart by hitting the sides with a hammer—the wood will split and be useless.

Note the correct way: place a block on the side so that blows of the hammer loosen the entire side without splitting.

Saw off the sides of the box next to the nails. This method insures good pieces of wood without splits or hammer marks.

A few suggestions are shown here for taking the boxes apart. Never hit the side of thin boxes, or fruit boxes, with a hammer. Nine times out of ten you will split the wood. Instead, select a heavy wood block as long as the boards are wide. When this block is struck with the hammer, the entire end of the board is loosened. You can also take boxes apart by sawing off the board near the end. The small ends remaining are removed and the nails withdrawn easily.

In studying the plans for the house you are going to build, look for parts that have the same dimensions, such as the front and back. Nail together the two pieces of stock for such parts, mark one of them, and cut out both at the same time. This not only saves time but also insures cutting the pieces to the same size. They can be cut by hand with a cross-cut saw or with a power jig saw. In drilling the entrance hole, use an expansive bit and set it accurately. To prevent splintering the wood on the far side, clamp the stock in the bench vise, using a back-up block as shown on page 127. The bit will enter the second block, cut a clean sharp hole in the front of the house, and there will be no ragged edge.

Vent holes are usually made with a ¼-inch drill. A drill press or ordinary portable drill can be used instead of a hand drill. As a rule, the grain of the front and back pieces

To make duplicate pieces, brad them together and saw both at the same time.

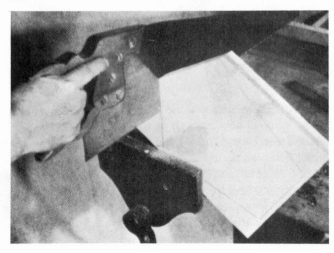

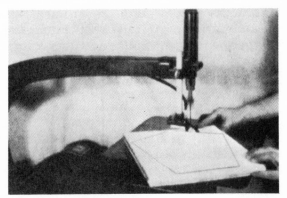

The use of a jig saw simplifies cutting of straight and curved pieces.

The drill press is used for boring all holes. Here vent holes are being made.

When boring the entrance hole with an expansive bit, place a scrap piece of wood in back of the hole to prevent splintering.

should run vertically. The grain for the sidepieces and roof pieces should run horizontally. Wherever possible, in order to make the cutting and fitting of the stock simple, the angles in the designs have been kept to simple degrees and values such as 45, 30, and 60 degrees. In a few cases other angles had to be used but they have been avoided if possible.

mounting the house

As already suggested, set up your birdhouse in the open, locating it where it will receive both light and shade. Be sure that there is no thick foliage nearby that can conceal enemies. At the same time, there should be trees reasonably close to serve as a perch. If possible, mount the birdhouse on a metal pole, preferably a 1-inch or 1¼-inch pipe. Set the pipe in the ground in either a rock-lined hole or in concrete.

Shown here are four practical, simple ways of mounting a typical birdhouse. If the house is to be suspended, use an eye bolt that extends through the roof and hang it by a long wire to provide protection from cats. If the house is mounted on pipe, screw a pipe flange the size of the pipe to the bottom of the house. For a flat mounting method, screw a strip to the back of the house, or drill a hole through the back opposite the front opening, and insert a long screw through the back.

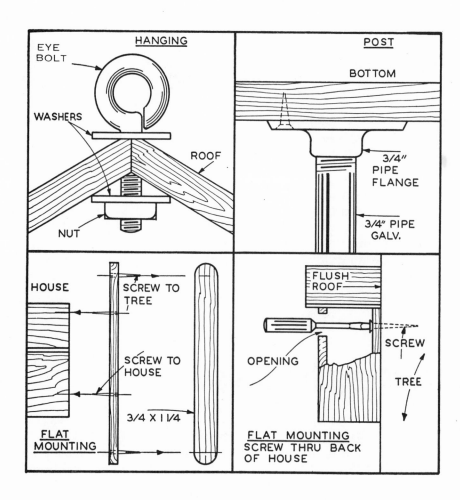

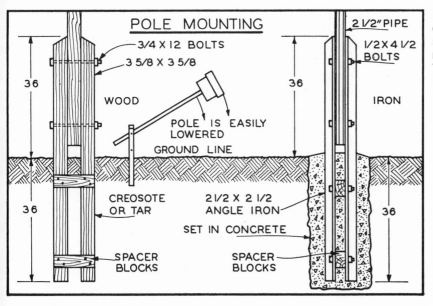

POLE MOUNTING

WOOD

3/4 X 12 BOLTS
3 5/8 X 3 5/8

36

36

CREOSOTE
OR TAR

SPACER
BLOCKS

POLE IS EASILY
LOWERED

GROUND LINE

2 1/2"PIPE
1/2 X 4 1/2 BOLTS

IRON

36

36

2 1/2 X 2 1/2
ANGLE IRON

SET IN CONCRETE

SPACER
BLOCKS

Here is a simple way to set wood or metal poles in the ground to support the heavy weight of the martin house. Use two bolts. The pole swings on one for easy lowering.

Shown above is a practical way of mounting heavy martin houses, using either a wood or metal pipe pole. For smaller, lighter houses you do not need poles as heavy as these, although it is a good idea to use this method of raising and lowering the house for cleaning.

Martin houses are commonly mounted on poles that can be lowered for cleaning. Either 4 by 4's or a pipe held between two angle irons set in concrete can be used. The two-bolt hanging arrangement allows one bolt to be taken out, usually the lower one, while the upper one acts as a pivot for lowering the house. The wooden house can be attached to the wood pole by means of iron angle brackets, or ornamental scroll brackets can be cut out of wood and bolted in place. A wire stretched to the pole holding the house or a nearby upright structure is often provided to give them a place to rest.

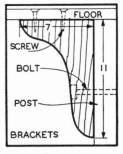

FLOOR
SCREW
BOLT
POST
BRACKETS

To fasten the wood martin house on the pole, make four wood brackets. Bolt them to the pole and screw on the martin house from inside.

squirrel and cat guard

A galvanized-iron protector in the shape of an inverted cone nailed to the post or bolted to the pipe will prevent squirrels and cats from getting at your feeder, or birdhouse. The funnel should extend at least 10 inches from the post.

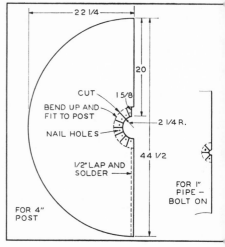

Shown and detailed is a typical installation. For mounting on pipe, the opening in the center must be smaller. To get an accurate fit, make a template out of paper or cardboard and then transfer it to the metal. Solder the ends of the metal together to avoid any ridges that would provide a foothold for squirrels.

tree guard

When hanging feeders or houses on tree branches, place a piece of split rubber garden house about the branch to prevent injury to the bark.

teeter-totter squirrel guard

The principle of this effective squirrel guard is that it "floats" on three evenly spaced supports. If a squirrel gets on the edge, the guard tips and he finds himself back on the ground! The tin must be lightweight—if it is too heavy, a squirrel can get onto it, for a moment, which is just long enough for it to jump to the feeder above. If the guard is light he cannot get a foothold. The diameter of the guard should be at least 20 inches. The hole in the center of the plate must be large enough to permit the plate to tip a full 45 degrees. For a 4-inch post the hole should be 5¾ inches; for ½-inch pipe, 1⅛ inches; for ¾-inch pipe, 1½ inches; and for 1 inch pipe, 1-13/16 inches.

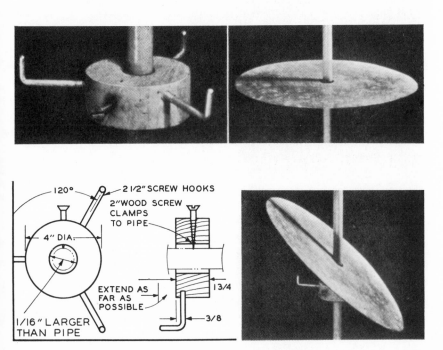

For mounting on a post, use three headless 5-inch spikes evenly spaced around the upright to support the plate. Have them extend out as far as possible. For mounting on a metal pipe or rod, cut out a ring of hardwood as shown. The ring is held to the pipe by means of the wood screw that protrudes into the center opening. The center opening should be: for ½-inch pipe, ⅞-inch; for ¾-inch pipe, 1⅛-inches and for 1-inch pipe, 1-5/16-inches. The best position of the guard on the post is just below the feeder, but be sure that it does not touch the bottom of the feeder when it tilts to 45 degrees. This is one of the best guard designs available and it is simple and easy to make.

a house for your bluebird lane

Recent studies and counts by the National Audubon Society and the U. S. Fish and Wildlife Service show that there is a marked decrease in the bluebird population. Bluebirds may even be faced with extinction if nothing is done to help this beneficial and beautiful species.

The reasons for the decline of this species are many. First, our effort to "clean up" woods, fence rows, and fields have led to a reduction in nesting facilities. Hollow trees are cut down and old cedar fence posts are replaced by metal posts. These old posts and trees also are a source of food and as they are destroyed food is also destroyed. An additional hazard to all bird life is the ever-increasing use of sprays for insect control.

To help restore the bluebird population, you can build a dozen or so houses of the type shown here. Use any sort of wood available. Stain the houses a dark green or brown if you want. Then select a "route" or lane and install them. A fence row is an ideal location. Or, if you can, set them up along the edge of a woods with open fields on one side. Mount them about 5 feet off the ground. Do not place them near barns or dwellings. Since each bird has a definite territory, place the houses about 500 yards apart.

Visit your "lane" from time to time and see how your tenants are getting along. You are sure to find families in several of them. If you do not succeed the first year, don't give up—they will be there the following year. At the end of the season clean out the houses and have them ready for spring. It will be a lot of fun.

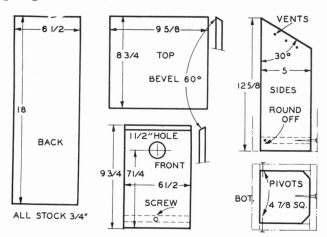

132

the covered-wagon wren house

The covered-wagon wren house is a simple birdhouse that any boy or girl can build. It makes an excellent school group project. Wood and roofing paper are used in its construction.

Make the two endpieces first. Cut them out with coping saw or on a scroll saw. Drill the ¾-inch hole and the ¼-inch hole in one end as indicated. Cut the bottom and nail the ends to it. Cut the top strip and nail it in place. Lay out the pattern for the roof on paper, trace it onto the roofing paper, and cut with tin shears. Tack the roof to the endpieces and insert a screw eye.

Paint the outside of the house to harmonize with the color of the roofing paper.

bill of materials

Ends:	2— ½ x 4 x 6 in.	
Bottom:	1— ½ x 3¼ x 3¼ in.	
Top strip:	1— ½ x ½ x 3¼ in.	
Roofing paper:	1—7 x 14½ in.	
Screw eye:	1— ¾ in. long	

WREN HOUSE

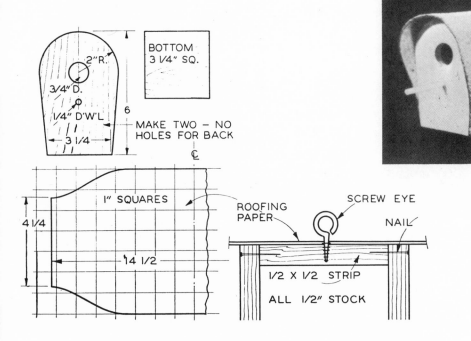

BOTTOM
3 1/4" SQ.

2" R.
3/4" D.
1/4" D'W'L
3 1/4
6
MAKE TWO — NO HOLES FOR BACK

1" SQUARES
4 1/4
14 1/2
ROOFING PAPER
SCREW EYE
NAIL
1/2 X 1/2 STRIP
ALL 1/2" STOCK

133

cedar-log wren house

For the cedar-log wren house, use a piece of green cedar post that does not have a tendency to check or crack when drying. To form the 3½-inch nest, first drill a series of holes around the outside; then drill out the rest of the wood the same way. Cut the slant at the top and drill the entrance hole as well as the hole for the ¼-inch dowel perch. Cut the roof and nail it in place.

The wren house can be left natural and the roof stained brown or green. Mount the house through the hole in the back of the house opposite the front opening.

bill of materials

Cedar log
for the body: 1—   5-in. dia. x 7½ in.
Roof: 1—½ x 6 x 7 in.
Dowel
for perch: 1—¼-in. dia. x 3 in.

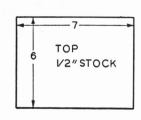

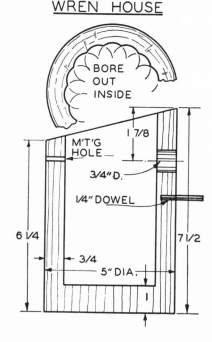

WREN HOUSE

four-square wren house

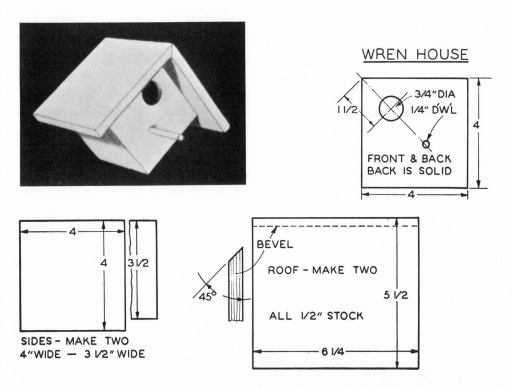

WREN HOUSE

3/4" DIA
1/4" DW'L

1 1/2

4

4

FRONT & BACK
BACK IS SOLID

4

SIDES – MAKE TWO
4" WIDE — 3 1/2" WIDE

4

4

3 1/2

BEVEL

ROOF – MAKE TWO

45°

5 1/2

ALL 1/2" STOCK

6 1/4

The four-square wren house is simple in design and unique in appearance. It also is a fine group project for the school shop. The ends are 4 inches square. Drill the ¾-inch dia. entrance and the ¼-inch perch hole in one end. Make both sidepieces 4 inches long but make one of them 3½ inches wide and the other 4 inches wide. Make the two roof boards the same dimensions and bevel them 45 degrees as indicated. Nail the bottom edge of sides together. Next nail on the ends and then the roof.

Paint the wren house white if desired with a contrasting red or green roof. Mount by means of a screw eye.

bill of materials

Ends:	2— ½ x 4 x 4 in.
Side:	1— ½ x 4 x 4 in.
Side:	1— ½ x 3½ x 4 in.
Roof:	2— ½ x 5½ x 6¼ in.
Dowel for perch:	1— ¼-in. dia. x 2 in.
Screw eye:	1—1 in. long

135

house wren shelter

This house wren shelter has an ever popular design of pleasing proportions. The construction is relatively simple because all cuts are straight with only one angle, namely, that of the sidepieces.

Cut the pieces for the sides and top to size. Nail on the front and back and then nail on the roof. Cut the bottom last and fit in place. Round off the rear bottom edge of the bottom so that it will swing freely. Drill pivot holes in the sides and insert brass screws through the holes and drive them into the bottom. Then put in the front screw which holds the bottom in place. Next fit the mounting strip in the back and notch out the roof as indicated. Be sure to make vent holes in the sides as shown on the drawing.

The house wren shelter can be stained or painted.

bill of materials

Sides:	2—½ x 5	x 6¼ in.	
Front:	1—½ x 6	x 6½ in.	
Back:	1—½ x 6	x 3⅜ in.	
Roof:	1—½ x 10	x 9½ in.	
Bottom:	1—½ x 5	x 5 in.	
Mounting strip:	1—¾ x 1¼ x 12	in.	

HOUSE WREN

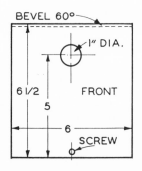

BEVEL 60°

1" DIA.

6 1/2

5

FRONT

6

SCREW

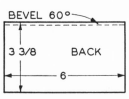

BEVEL 60°

3 3/8   BACK

6

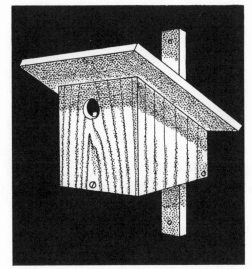

ALL STOCK
1/2"

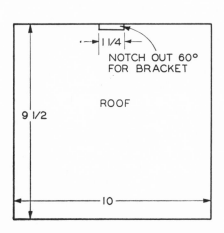

1 1/4

NOTCH OUT 60°
FOR BRACKET

ROOF

9 1/2

10

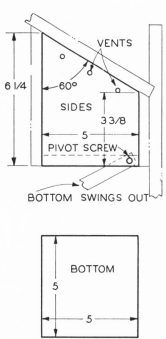

VENTS

6 1/4

60°

SIDES

3 3/8

5

PIVOT SCREW

BOTTOM SWINGS OUT

BOTTOM

5

5

3/4 X 1 1/4 X 12 BRACKET

bluebird house

Every bird fancier will want this house to attract bluebirds to his yard and garden. It has an attractive design and at the same time meets all the specifications for a bluebird house. The scrolled eaves lend charm to this fine bird dwelling.

Make the front and back at the same time by nailing the stock for them together and cutting them to size in one operation. Drill the entrance hole in the front piece. Cut the perch supports and nail them on the front with the dowel cross bar before you start to assemble the house.

Cut the other pieces to size. Nail the front and back to the sidepieces. Now nail on the roof boards. Then cut the decorative eaves on the scroll saw or with a coping saw, two at a time. Note that the top must have the same pitch as the roof, namely, 60 degrees on each side of center line. Nail the eaves to the roof in front and back ½ inch from the edge.

Now cut and fit the bottom. Round off the rear bottom edge of the bottom so it will swing clear for cleaning. Drill holes for the side pivot brass screws and then drive in these screws and the front holding screw. Use an eye bolt to mount this bluebird house as described on page 128.

Stain or paint the house as desired. The roof can be a contrasting color.

bill of materials

Front and back:	2— ½ x 9½ x 10⅝ in.
Sides:	2— ½ x 5 x 8 in.
Perch supports:	2— ½ x 2 x 4½ in.
Dowel for perch:	1— ¼-in. dia. dowel x 7 in. long
Roof:	2— ½ x 7½ x 10 in.
Bottom:	1—4½ x 5 in.
Scroll eaves:	2— ½ x 3½ x 10½ in.

BLUEBIRD

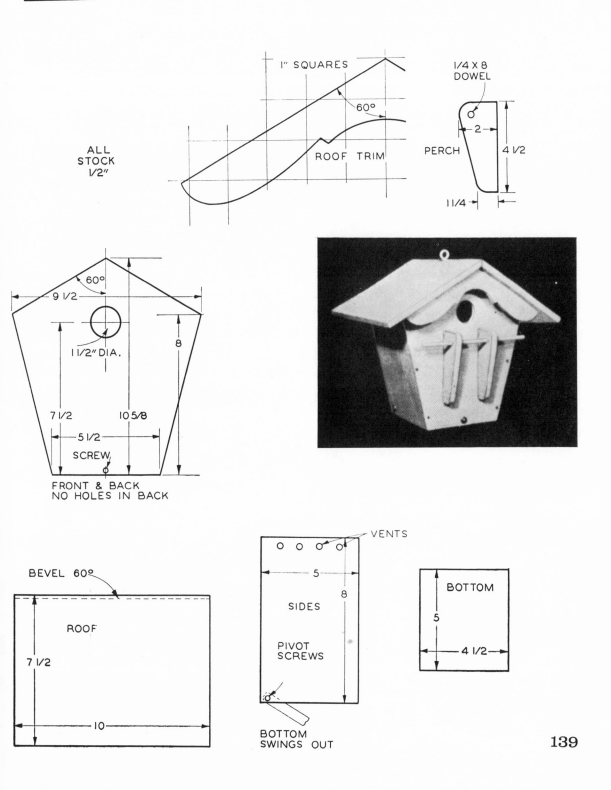

1" SQUARES

60°

ROOF TRIM

ALL
STOCK
1/2"

1/4 X 8
DOWEL

PERCH

2

4 1/2

1 1/4

60°

9 1/2

1 1/2" DIA.

8

7 1/2

10 5/8

5 1/2

SCREW

FRONT & BACK
NO HOLES IN BACK

BEVEL 60°

ROOF

7 1/2

10

VENTS

5

SIDES

8

PIVOT
SCREWS

BOTTOM
SWINGS OUT

BOTTOM

5

4 1/2

139

house for a tree swallow
or violet green swallow

The house shown on the opposite page offers a challenge to the craftsman since it requires compound angles at all the corners. If made by hand the sides must be beveled at angles of 54 degrees for the wall joints and 51 degrees for the roof. Square up the pieces and then bevel the edges.

If a circular saw is available, you can expedite the job by setting the saw and miter gauge as indicated and sawing the pieces on a production basis. For the side walls, tilt the saw 41¾ degrees and set the miter gauge 71¼ degrees if the gauge in the normal position reads 90 degrees. Boards 7 inches wide can then be beveled to the correct angle.

Repeat this operation for the four roof boards but set the saw and the miter gauge at the required angles. It is suggested that you run through a piece of scrap wood as a check before making the final cuts.

Drill the entrance in one side. Assemble the body of the house part and then the roof and nail together. Then cut and fit the bottom. Drill the holes for the brass pivot screws on both sides and screw them in place. Then drive in the front holding screw.

Mount the house by using a screw bolt with washers top and bottom as explained on page 128. The house can be painted or stained.

bill of materials

Sides:	4—½ x 10¾ x 7 in.
Roof:	4—½ x 12¾ x 12¾ in.
Bottom:	1—½ x 5 x 5 in.
Screw bolt:	1—¼-in. dia. x 4 in.

140

TREE SWALLOW
VIOLET GREEN
SWALLOW

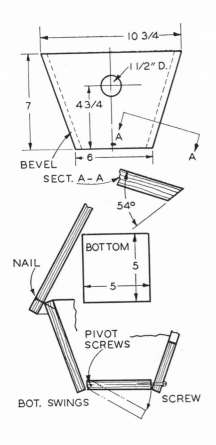

10 3/4

1 1/2" D.

4 3/4

7

6

BEVEL

SECT. A-A

54°

A

A

NAIL

BOTTOM

5

5

PIVOT
SCREWS

BOT. SWINGS

SCREW

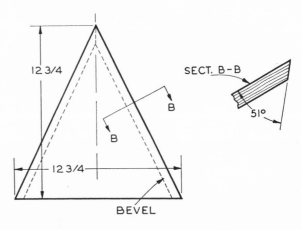

12 3/4

12 3/4

SECT. B-B

51°

B

B

BEVEL

ALL STOCK 1/2"

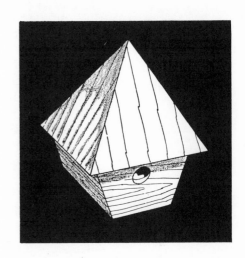

TO CUT ON CIRCULAR SAW :

	TILT SAW A°	MIT. GAUGE B
ROOF	37 3/4°	63 1/2°
SIDES	41 3/4°	71 1/4°

SET OF
MITER
GAUGE

90°

0°

B

A°

TILT OF CIRCULAR SAW

141

flicker house

The design and dimensions of this flicker house are especially tailored to meet the requirements of this interesting bird. The swing-out bottom makes it easy to clean. The roof is flush in back for mounting against a tree or a building.

Only the front has the ornamental design. Make the front first and then the back, taking care that the roof angles are the same. Then cut the other pieces. Nail the back to the side pieces. Then nail on the front after the perch brackets have been nailed on from the inside. Keep the house square. Nail on the two roof boards and then the ornamental scroll eaves at the front. The roof is flush with the back. The eaves set back 1 inch from the front edge.

Cut and fit the bottom. Drill a hole on both sides for the pivot screw. Round off the bottom back edge of the bottom so that it swings free. Hold it in place with two brass pivot screws, one on each side, and the holding screw in front. Mount the house through a hole in the back or by means of a mounting strip extending from the top to the bottom and screwed on from the back.

Stain the house a deep brown or dark green.

bill of materials

Front:	1—½ x 9½ x 18½ in.
Back:	1—½ x 6¾ x 15 in.
Sides:	2—½ x 6½ x 13 in.
Roof:	2—½ x 7½ x 10 in.
Bottom:	1—½ x 5¾ x 6½ in.
Perch brackets:	2—½ x 1¾ x 4½ in.
Dowel for perch:	1—¼-in. dia. x 7 in.
Ornamental eave:	1—½ x 3½ x 10½ in.

FLICKER HOUSE

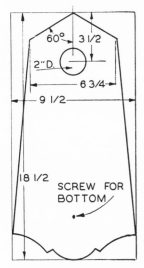

60°   3 1/2
2"D.
6 3/4
9 1/2
18 1/2
SCREW FOR BOTTOM

ALL 1/2" STOCK

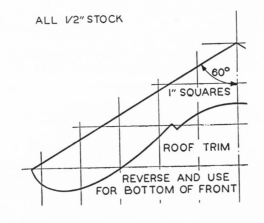

60°
1" SQUARES
ROOF TRIM
REVERSE AND USE
FOR BOTTOM OF FRONT

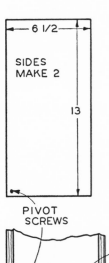

6 1/2
SIDES MAKE 2
13
PIVOT SCREWS

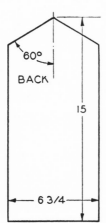

60°
BACK
15
6 3/4

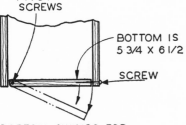

BOTTOM IS 5 3/4 X 6 1/2
SCREW
BOTTOM SWINGS FOR CLEANING

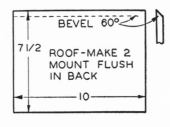

BEVEL 60°
7 1/2   ROOF-MAKE 2
MOUNT FLUSH IN BACK
10

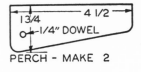

1 3/4   4 1/2
1/4" DOWEL
PERCH - MAKE 2

chickadee split-log house

Shop students and homecraftsmen have a lot of fun constructing a split-log chickadee house, although it requires a considerable amount of handwork. However, when this model is made with care, the final product is a unique house that is well worth the effort.

Select any solid check-free log about 6 inches in diameter and 12 inches long. Use elm, pine, spruce, or any similar wood. Do not use one of the hardwoods because it would be difficult to gouge out the inside.

If a band saw is available, split the log as shown or cut it by hand with a ripsaw. To keep the log from rolling while you are sawing, nail two 45-degree strips on the bottom as shown. Be sure the nails are not in the path of the saw. The saw blade will not pinch and cutting will be made safe.

Gouge out the two halves after they have been marked. In one half drill the 1⅛-inch entrance hole. In the other half, opposite the entrance hole, drill the hole for the mounting screw. Now tie the two halves together with a piece of rope and put them in accurate alignment. Drill the four screw holes and screw the two pieces together, using brass screws. The holes may be plugged if desired. Cut the top even and nail the roof on the rear half of the house. Do not nail it onto the front because the front may be removed by loosening the four screws for cleaning the house.

No stain or paint is needed.

bill of materials

Log for body:	1—6-in. dia. x 12 in.
Roof (slab with bark):	1—7 in. x 7 in.
Brass screws:	4—2½ in. long

CHICKADEE

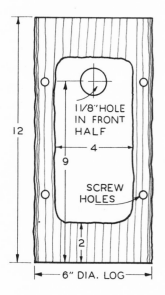

1 1/8" HOLE IN FRONT HALF

12

4

9

SCREW HOLES

2

6" DIA. LOG

GOUGE OUT BY HAND

SPLIT LOG ON BAND SAW

ROOF:
BARK SLAB, 7 X 7

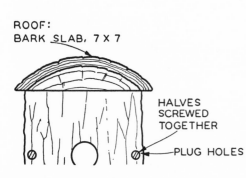

HALVES SCREWED TOGETHER

PLUG HOLES

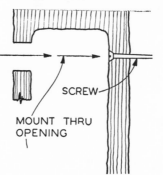

SCREW

MOUNT THRU OPENING

145

downy woodpecker
rustic log house

This downy woodpecker house is another split log house that is quite simple to make but requires a little more handwork than the average birdhouse. However, these rustic houses always lend a special charm to the yard or garden where they are used.

Select a softwood log such as pine, spruce, or cedar that is solid and free of checks and has the bark adhering to it. The log should be 6 inches in diameter and 14 inches long. Split it on a band saw as shown on page 145 or cut it by hand with the ripsaw. With a gouge and mallet hollow out both halves from top to bottom, making the depression about 4 inches in diameter.

Now put the two halves together and tie rope around them so they cannot move. Drill the four holes and fasten the pieces together with brass screws 2 ½ inches long. Remove the rope. Then fit in a ¾-inch round wood bottom held in place with wood screws so that it can be easily removed for cleaning. Drill the entrance hole and the hole for the ⅜-inch dowel perch. Cut the top for the roof at a 55-degree angle and nail on the roof boards.

The roof can be stained dark brown or green. Mount the house by means of screws driven through the back and into a block nailed to a tree. The block is necessary to accommodate the roof which has an overhang in the back.

bill of materials

Log for body:	1—6 in. in dia. x 14 in.
Bottom:	1—¾ x approx. 4-in. dia.
Roof:	2—¾ x 8 x 8 in.
Dowel for perch:	1—⅜ in. dia. x 3½ in.
Brass screws:	4—2½ in. long

DOWNY
WOODPECKER

ROOF: 3/4" STOCK
8 X 8

BEVEL 55°

8

55°

1 1/4" DIA.

10 1/2

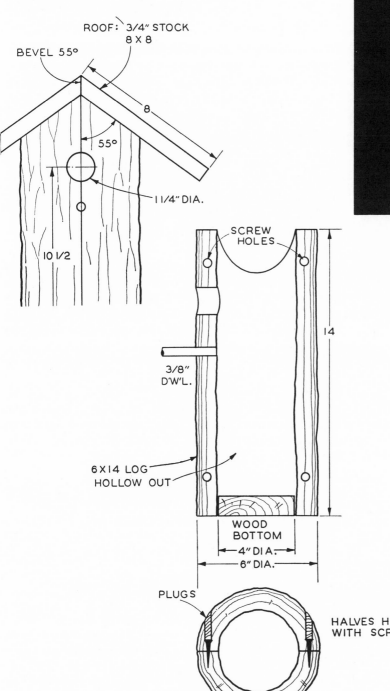

SCREW
HOLES

14

3/8"
D'W'L.

6 X 14 LOG
HOLLOW OUT

WOOD
BOTTOM

4" DIA.

6" DIA.

PLUGS

HALVES HELD TOGETHER
WITH SCREWS

red-headed and hairy woodpecker six-sided house

A power jointer facilitates the building of this woodpecker house since the 60-degree bevel on the sides can be accurately and easily produced on this machine. However, good joints can be made by hand and it is a proof of skill to make the beveled edges even and fit snugly.

Cut the six sidepieces to the same dimensions and bevel the edges. In one piece, which will be the front, bore the 2-inch diameter entrance hole. Nail the six pieces together by double toenailing. Cut and fit in the six-sided bottom. Hold it in place with three brass wood screws, 1 inch long. This method of attachment allows it to be removed for easy cleaning.

Now set the house down on its back and mark off the 60-degree pitch of the roof on the front. Cut the sides to this slant for the roof. Make the roof boards and nail them in place.

Stain the house dark brown with weatherproof stain. Since the roof is flush in back, it can be mounted by screw through the back as shown on the drawing.

bill of materials

Sides:	6—¾ x 4⅜ x 18	in.
Bottom:	1—¾ x 6 x 6⅞	in.
Roof:	2—¾ x 9 x 9	in.

REDHEADED WOODPECKER
HAIRY WOODPECKER

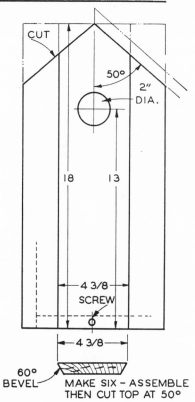

CUT

50°

2" DIA.

18   13

4 3/8
SCREW

4 3/8

60°
BEVEL

MAKE SIX – ASSEMBLE
THEN CUT TOP AT 50°

ALL STOCK 3/4"

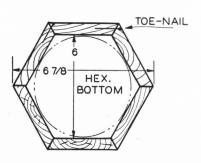

TOE-NAIL

6

6 7/8   HEX.
BOTTOM

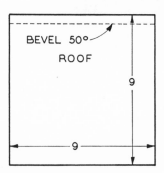

BEVEL 50°
ROOF

9

9

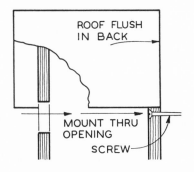

ROOF FLUSH
IN BACK

MOUNT THRU
OPENING
SCREW

149

titmouse house

The pleasing lines of this titmouse house have made it the favorite of many bird attractors. This house is an excellent one to adapt for other birds by altering the size of the opening, the depth, and the inside dimensions to accommodate them.

Nail together the stock for the front and back pieces, and cut these parts at the same time. Make the entrance hole in the front. Now carefully lay out the side pieces, duplicating the scroll design on the front edge. These parts, too, can be nailed together for cutting in order to produce exactly matching pieces.

Nail the sides onto the back and then nail the front in place. Next nail on the roof boards. Cut the bottom and round off the bottom top edge so that the bottom will swing free for cleaning. Drill the holes for the pivot screws in the sides. Use brass screws to hold the bottom in place. Put another brass screw in the front. Screw the mounting bracket on the back.

Give the house a coat of waterproof brown stain.

bill of materials

Front and back:	2—½ x 4 x 10½ in.
Sides:	2—½ x 6¾ x 9 in.
Roof:	2—½ x 5½ x 7¼ in.
Bottom:	1—½ x 4 x 4 in.
Mounting bracket:	1—¾ x 1½ x 18 in.
Dowel for perch:	1—¼ in. dia. x 9 in.

TITMOUSE

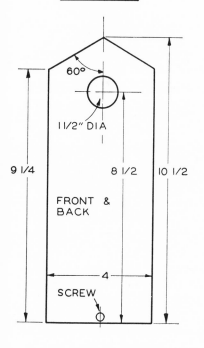

60°

11/2" DIA

9 1/4

8 1/2

10 1/2

FRONT & BACK

4

SCREW

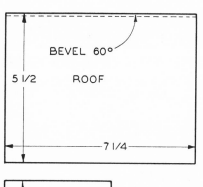

BEVEL 60°

5 1/2   ROOF

7 1/4

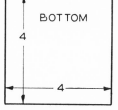

BOTTOM

4

4

ALL STOCK 1/2"

3/4 X 11/2 X 18 MOUNTING BR'K'T

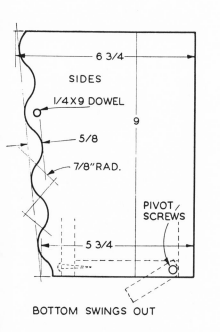

6 3/4

SIDES

1/4 X 9 DOWEL

5/8

7/8" RAD.

9

PIVOT SCREWS

5 3/4

BOTTOM SWINGS OUT

151

location suggestions

The question is often asked: where is the best place to mount and locate a bird house? The answer is: never locate it in deep shade or thick foliage. Place the house in partial shade so that it is kept cool, out of the sun's hot rays. However, do not select heavy foliage because enemies of birds may hide there and the birds will be wary of it. A few dead branches near the house will afford good perches.

robin shelf

Anyone can make a robin shelf which is as simple in construction as the one shown here. Although the supporting brackets are scrolled, they can be made straight if you do not want the curved cuts.

Make all the pieces according to the specifications on the drawing. Nail the roof on the back and then nail in the roof supporting brackets from the back and top. Next nail on the bottom and then the side brackets to complete the shelf.

Give the robin shelf a coat of weatherproof stain. It might also be painted dark green or brown.

This robin shelf can be mounted under the eaves of a house or garage or in some other protected place. Never place it in the direct sun or in the open. As an added feature, small pegs can be installed in the top surface of the bottom to act as anchors for the nest. These pegs can be ¼-inch dowels extending ¾ inches to 1 inch above the floor.

bill of materials

Back:	1—½ x 8½ x 9½ in.
Roof:	1—½ x 7½ x 10½ in.
Bottom:	1—½ x 8½ x 7½ in.
Top supporting brackets:	2—½ x 4¼ x 6½ in.
Side brackets:	2—½ x 2 x 6½ in.

ROBIN SHELF

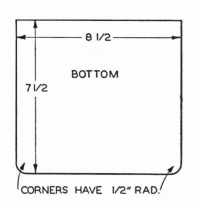

BOTTOM

8 1/2

7 1/2

CORNERS HAVE 1/2" RAD.

ALL STOCK 1/2"

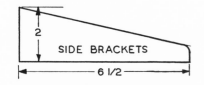

2

SIDE BRACKETS

6 1/2

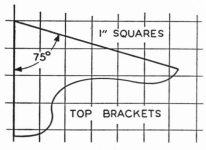

1" SQUARES

75°

TOP BRACKETS

7 1/2

ROOF

10 1/2

BEVEL 15°

8 1/2

BACK

9 1/2

153

nuthatch house

This nuthatch house is of an old design but it is one that is always well liked. Perhaps the reason for its popularity is due to the fact that while the house has an elaborate appearance it is very simple to build. It requires a minimum of stock and consists of only a few parts.

Nail together the stock for the front and the back and cut the pieces at the same time. Then bore the entrance hole in the front piece. Next make the roof and nail on the front and back.

Cut and fit the bottom accurately. Hold it in place with two brass screws in front and two in back as indicated. If screws are used for this purpose, the house can be easily cleaned. The house can be mounted on a ¾-inch pipe flange and on a pipe as shown on page 128, or the screw-bolt mounting method may be used.

Stain or paint house but use a dark color.

bill of materials

Front and		
back:	2—½ x 9⅛ x 8	in.
Roof:	2—½ x 11½ x 11½	in.
Bottom:	1—½ x 8½ x 8½	in.

NUTHATCH

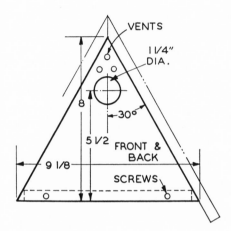

VENTS

1 1/4"
DIA.

8

30°

5 1/2   FRONT &
          BACK

9 1/8

SCREWS

ALL STOCK
1/2"

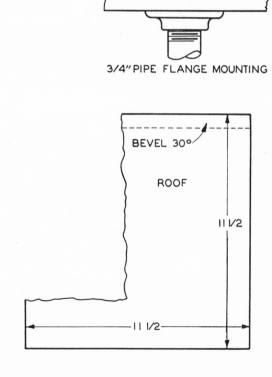

3/4" PIPE FLANGE MOUNTING

BEVEL 30°

ROOF

11 1/2

11 1/2

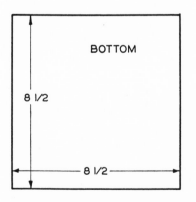

BOTTOM

8 1/2

8 1/2

house finch—shelter I

Although this finch house is quite simple to assemble, the roof notches in the front and back pieces must be accurately made and do present a challenge to the builder.

Lay out the front full size on a piece of paper. Transfer this layout to the stock either by tracing or by attaching the paper to the stock with cellophane tape. Nail together the stock for the front and back and cut them out at the same time so that the roof and side pieces will fit tight. Bore the hole in the frontpiece. Now cut the other pieces.

To assemble, first nail the front and back to the side pieces. Now nail on the lower roof pieces and finish with the beveled ridge pieces. Drill holes for the brass pivot screws on both sides. Round off the bottom rear edge of bottom so that it will swing clear for cleaning. Screw in the pivot screws. Install another brass holding screw in the front after drilling a hole for it.

Stain or paint the house using dull, dark colors.

The finch house can be mounted on a pipe flange and galvanized pipe.

bill of materials

Front and back:	2—½ x 9½ x	9⅛ in.
Sides:	2—½ x 6 x	6 in.
Roof:	6—½ x 2½ x	10 in.
Ridge:	2—½ x 2 x	10 in.
Bottom:	1—½ x 6 x	6 in.

HOUSE FINCH

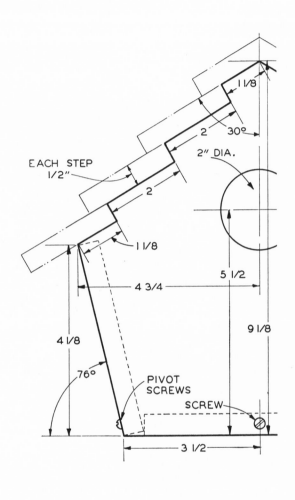

EACH STEP
1/2"

1 1/8

2   30°

2" DIA.

2

1 1/8

5 1/2

4 3/4

9 1/8

4 1/8

76°

PIVOT
SCREWS

SCREW

3 1/2

ALL STOCK
1/2"

FRONT AND BACK
NO HOLES IN BACK

MAKE LAYOUT ON
PAPER — TRACE ON
STOCK

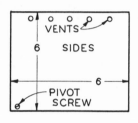

VENTS

6   SIDES

6

6

PIVOT
SCREW

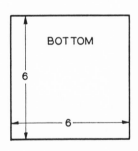

BOTTOM

6

6

BEVEL 60°

2   RIDGE BOARDS - MAKE TWO
10

ROOF BOARDS - MAKE SIX
2 1/2
10

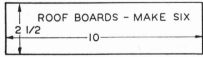

house finch—shelter II

The squat appearance of this finch house is sure to attract attention. The house is simple to build although the angles of the front and back pieces must be accurately cut.

Nail the stock for the front and back pieces together so that you can cut them out at the same time. Bore the entrance hole in the front piece. Then make the other parts. Now nail the front and back to the side pieces; then nail on the roof. The bottom swings out on two pivot screws on the sides. Drill the sides for the brass pivot screws as indicated. Round off the bottom rear edge of the bottom to provide clearance. Next put another brass screw in the front to hold the bottom.

The house can be painted or stained as desired. Mount it on a pipe flange and galvanized pipe as indicated.

bill of materials

Front and back:	2—½ x 8 x 12 in.
Sides:	2—½ x 4¾ x 7 in.
Roof:	2—½ x 10 x 11 in.
Bottom:	1—½ x 6⅛ x 7 in.

HOUSE
FINCH

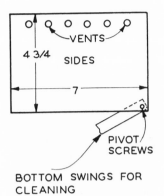

VENTS

4 3/4   SIDES

7

PIVOT
SCREWS

BOTTOM SWINGS FOR
CLEANING

ALL STOCK 1/2"

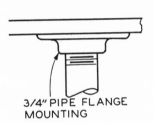

3/4" PIPE FLANGE
MOUNTING

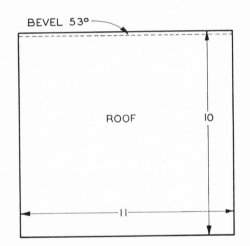

53°   2" DIA.

8

5

12

3 1/2   SCREW

90°

54°

BEVEL 53°

ROOF

10

11

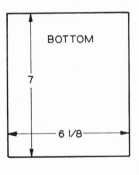

BOTTOM

7

6 1/8

159

song sparrow shelf

Although the shelter featured here is called a shelf, it really is a house without walls and is very much to the liking of the song sparrow.

Make the four corner posts as shown in the drawing and notch out the tops accurately for the front and back gables. Cut the gables and nail to the corner posts. Then from below, nail the posts to the floor, which is ¾-inch stock. As the last operation, nail on the two roof boards.

The house can be painted white, if desired, or any other color that is suitable. Mount it on a post one to three feet from the ground.

If you want, you can add several pegs in the floor to act as anchors to keep the nest from blowing or sliding off. These can be ¼-inch dia. dowels by ¾-inch long.

bill of materials

Posts:	4—1 x 1 x 5½ in.	
Gables:	2—½ x 2¼ x 7 in.	
Floor:	1—¾ x 7 x 7 in.	
Roof:	2—½ x 6¼ x 11 in.	

SONG
SPARROW

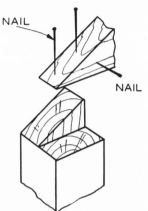

NAIL

NAIL

GABLES
1/2" STOCK

2 1/4   60°

7

BEVEL 60°

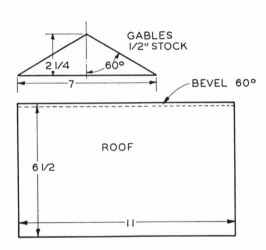

ROOF

6 1/2

11

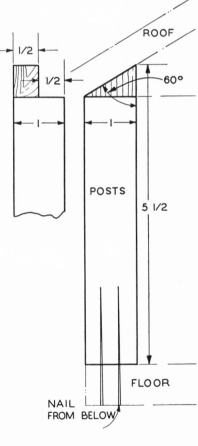

ROOF

1/2

1/2

1

60°

1

POSTS

5 1/2

FLOOR

NAIL
FROM BELOW

7

FLOOR

7

3/4" STOCK

161

phoebe and barn swallow shelf

This shelf is designed for the phoebe and barn swallow, but is also used by the robin. Two sides are completely open; the third is almost closed. Cut all the pieces as per drawing. As the first step in assembling the shelf, nail the back to the floor. Then nail on the side and finally the roof. The construction work involved is very simple. Paint the shelf white or any other suitable color. Mount it in a secluded and protected place.

162

bill of materials

Back:	1—½ x 7 x 13¾ in.
Side:	1—½ x 4¾ x 9½ in.
Floor:	1—½ x 6 x 7 in.
Roof:	1—½ x 7½ x 7 in.

PHOEBE AND
BARN SWALLOW

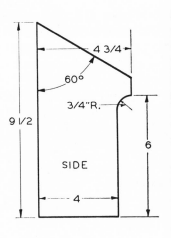

SIDE

4 3/4
60°
3/4"R.
9 1/2
6
4

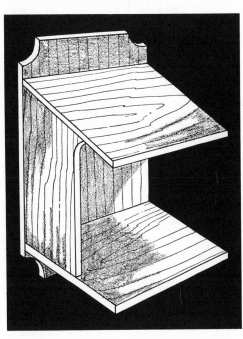

ALL
STOCK
1/2"

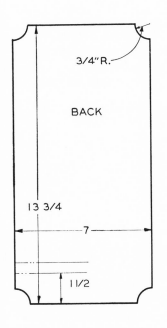

3/4"R.
BACK
13 3/4
7
1 1/2

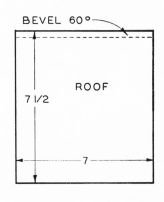

BEVEL 60°
ROOF
7 1/2
7

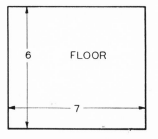

6
FLOOR
7

163

barn owl house

Can we fool the barn owl and have him make his nest in this house just because it is the shape of a barn? Whatever his preferences, this novel house provides enough room for the large nest that the owl builds.

Nail together the stock for the front and back and cut them at the same time. Be sure that your dimensions are accurate. Cut the large 6-inch diameter opening in the front with a coping saw or a scroll saw. Then cut the other pieces.

To assemble, nail the sides to the bottom; then nail on the front and back after the perch has been nailed to the front piece. The perch is made out of one half of the part cut out for the entrance opening. Next, nail on the lower roof pieces and then nail on the upper or ridge roof pieces. The bottom of this house does not swing out because the opening is large enough for easy cleaning.

Paint or stain house with weatherproof materials. Any color is suitable.

bill of materials

Front and back:	2—½ x 9½ x 12¾ in.	
Sides:	2—½ x 7¾ x 17	in.
Bottom:	1—½ x 8½ x 17	in.
Lower roof parts:	2—½ x 4 x 20	in.
Upper roof parts:	2—½ x 5 x 20	in.
Perch:	1—½-in. x 3 in.	
	(½ of the cutout from the entrance)	

BARN
OWL

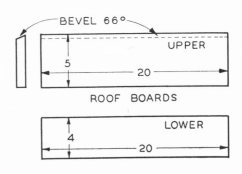

BEVEL 66°

UPPER

5

20

ROOF BOARDS

LOWER

4

20

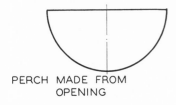

PERCH MADE FROM
OPENING

NO OPENING IN BACK

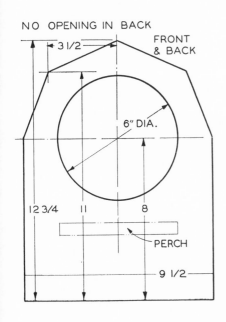

3 1/2

FRONT
& BACK

6" DIA.

12 3/4   11   8

PERCH

9 1/2

SIDES

7 3/4

17

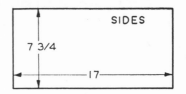

ALL STOCK 1/2"

BOTTOM

8 1/2

17

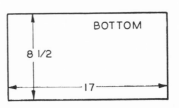

wood duck house

Extensive research on the habits and shelter of the wood duck has been conducted by Mr. Frank C. Bellrose, Associate Game Specialist of the Natural History Division of the State of Illinois at Urbana, Illinois, and all of the information given here is from Circular 45 printed by the division.

The house shown is the best developed to date for the protection of the wood duck. The top and sides are covered with tin so that squirrels cannot enter. The elliptical hole keeps out raccoons. The house is thus made predator proof. The best wood to use is rough-cut cypress. Cheaper lumber is suggested for the parts to be covered with the metal.

Make the roof of four triangular pieces with the edges beveled to 60-degree angles and toenailed together as shown in the drawing. Mount the pyramid-shaped assembly on a solid board. Cover the entire front and half of both sides with sheet metal. Next make the other parts of the box having one side hinged to provide easy cleaning. Make the hinged side fit tight to prevent light from entering the house. Cover both the sides and the front with sheet metal. Drill holes in the bottom for drainage.

If the house is to be finished, stain it dark brown. Do not use light or bright colors.

Cover the bottom with 2 or 3 inches of sawdust, shavings, or wood chips to provide a base for the nest. Mount the house on the side of a tree not more than a few hundred yards from water and about 10 to 25 feet above the ground. If you are planning to put up several, have the shelters 50 to 100 feet apart since the wood duck likes to nest in groups.

bill of materials

Roof:	4—	¾ x 18	x 12¾	in.
Roof floor:	1—	¾ x 18	x 18	in.
Front and back:	2—	¾ x 12	x 24	in.
Sides:	2—	¾ x 10½	x 24	in.
Bottom:	1—	¾ x 10½	x 10½	in.
Sheet metal:				
Top:	1—13½	x 25½ in.		
Front:	1—14	x 24	in.	
Sides:	2—12	x 24	in.	
Hinges (with screws)	2— 2	x 2	in.	

WOOD DUCK

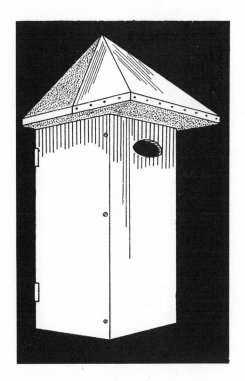

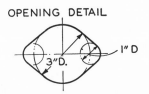

OPENING DETAIL

1" D

3" D.

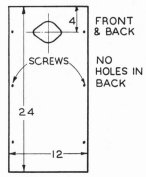

FRONT & BACK

4

SCREWS

NO HOLES IN BACK

24

12

COVER FRONT WITH GALV.
SHEET IRON 12" X 24"

ROOF MAKE 4

35°

BEVEL 60°

12 3/4

BEVEL 45°

18

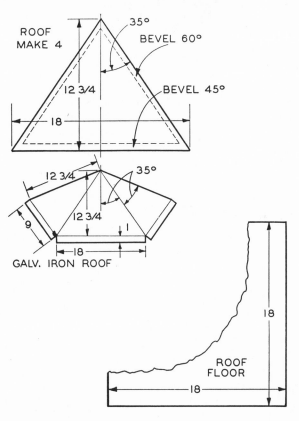

12 3/4

35°

12 3/4

9

18

1

GALV. IRON ROOF

2 X 2 HINGES

10 1/2

24

SIDES

ALL STOCK 3/4"

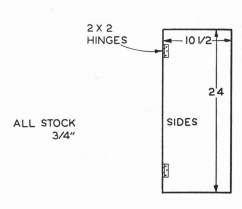

18

ROOF FLOOR

18

10 1/2

BOT'M.

DRAIN HOLES

10 1/2

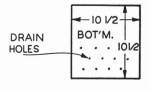

167

cupola 24-family martin house

This martin house has established itself as a shelter of pleasing proportions and design so it will certainly be a welcome sight on the roof on which it is installed. A good place for it is on the garage roof.

24-FAMILY MARTIN HOUSE

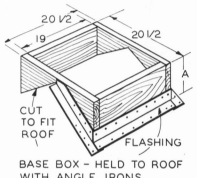

20 1/2
19
20 1/2
A

CUT TO FIT ROOF

FLASHING

BASE BOX – HELD TO ROOF WITH ANGLE IRONS

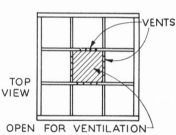

VENTS

TOP VIEW

OPEN FOR VENTILATION

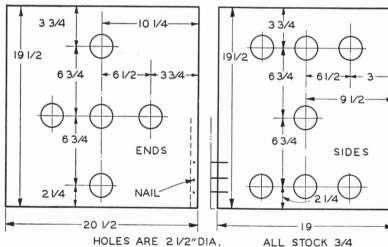

3 3/4
10 1/4
19 1/2
6 3/4
6 1/2
3 3/4
6 3/4
ENDS
2 1/4
NAIL

20 1/2
HOLES ARE 2 1/2" DIA.

3 3/4
19 1/2
6 3/4
6 1/2
3
9 1/2
6 3/4
SIDES
2 1/4

19
ALL STOCK 3/4

The lower base box can be eliminated and the house mounted on a 4 by 4-inch wood post or galvanized iron pipe. For this large house, use ¾-inch outside plywood with ¾-inch pine for the porches.

Make the base box first. Work with care so that it is perfectly level. Cut the sides to fit the angle of the roof. Install the metal roof flashings as indicated on the drawing and use roofing compound to seal all possible leaks.

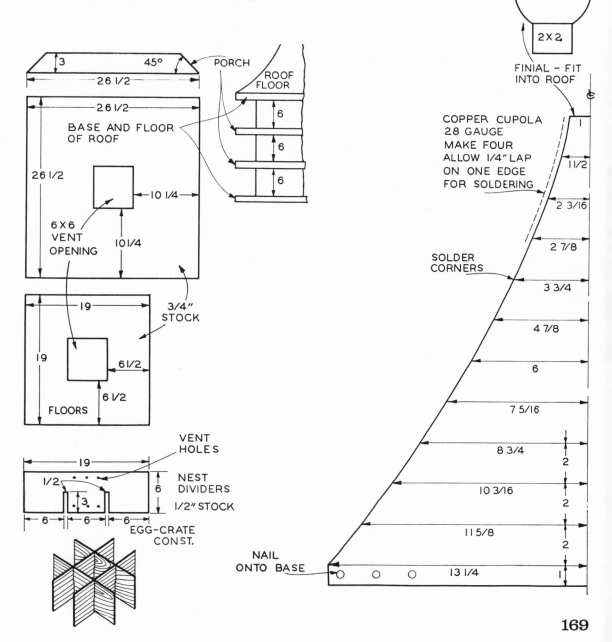

PORCH

ROOF FLOOR

3
45°
26 1/2

26 1/2

BASE AND FLOOR OF ROOF

6

6

6

26 1/2

10 1/4

6 X 6 VENT OPENING

10 1/4

3/4" STOCK

19

19

61/2

61/2

FLOORS

VENT HOLES

19

1/2

3

6

NEST DIVIDERS

1/2" STOCK

6

6

6

EGG-CRATE CONST.

NAIL ONTO BASE

4"DIA

2 X 2

FINIAL – FIT INTO ROOF

COPPER CUPOLA 28 GAUGE MAKE FOUR ALLOW 1/4" LAP ON ONE EDGE FOR SOLDERING

1

1 1/2

2 3/16

2 7/8

SOLDER CORNERS

3 3/4

4 7/8

6

7 5/16

8 3/4

2

10 3/16

2

11 5/8

2

13 1/4

1

Next cut the side pieces and assemble them on the base. Nail on the porches from the inside and toenail the corners. Then make the egg-crate nest dividers and the two floors. Assemble these in the house. The center of the house is open from top to bottom to provide the ventilation that is necessary to keep the house cool. The floors and dividers are removable for easy cleaning. Do not make them fit too tight.

Cut the copper for the roof. If copper is too expensive or not available, use galvanized sheet metal. Solder the corners. Fit the block into the top end to hold the finial ball. Mount the metal roof on the square roof floor.

The roof section is held to the main part of the house with angle irons and screws so that it may be easily removed for cleaning.

Paint the house white or paint it to match the building on which it is mounted.

bill of materials

Base sides:	2—¾ x 19 in. and wide enough to take the slant of the roof.	Sides:	2—¾ x 19	x 19½ in.
Base ends:	2—¾ x 20½ in. and wide enough to take the slant of the roof.	Base and floor of roof:	2—¾ x 26½ x 26½ in.	
		Floors:	2—¾ x 19	x 19 in.
		Dividers:	12—½ x 6	x 19 in.
		Porches:	8—¾ x 3	x 26½ in.
Metal flash-ing:	3 x 3 in. to fit around the base.	Finial:	1—4-in. dia.	
		Finial block:	1—2 x 2 x 2 in.	
House Ends:	2—¾ x 20½ x 19½ in.	Copper:	4—28 gauge x 27 x	23 in.

14-family martin house

This 14-family martin house, with its wide porches and corner posts has a southern colonial appearance.

Since the construction of the house is a sizable project, you can justify the purchase of outdoor weatherproof ¾-inch plywood for it, with the exception of the porches and the posts which are white pine. The entire attic portion is a separate unit and is attached to the main part of the house by iron angle brackets. It can be readily removed for easy cleaning of the house.

Make the bottom and attic floor, and then the sides. Assemble the sides and nail them to the bottom from below. Then make the posts and assemble them on the outside of the house with the porch. To add more grace to the house, the corner posts may be turned on the lathe as detailed.

Now make the inside floor and the egg-crate nest dividers. Small cleat blocks can be nailed to the floors to keep the dividers in place. Cut the gables and the center partition for the attic next: there are two apartments in the attic with openings at both ends. Mount the gables on the attic floor board and then nail the two roof boards in place. The ridge can be covered with tin or roofing paper. Use angle irons to attach the attic section to the main part of the house.

Paint the martin house white. Screw a large pipe flange on the bottom and mount the house on a galvanized iron pipe.

bill of materials

Bottom and attic floor:	2—	¾ x 20 x 26½ in.
Sides:	2—	¾ x 12½ x 19 in.
Ends:	2—	¾ x 14 x 12½ in.
Posts:	8—1¼ x	1¼ x 5⅞ in.
Porches:	2—	¾ x 3 x 26½ in.
Porches:	2—	¾ x 3 x 20 in.
Floor:	1—	¾ x 12½ x 19 in.
Nest dividers:	2—	½ x 6 x 19 in.
Nest dividers:	4—	½ x 6 x 12½ in.
Gables:	3—	¾ x 5¾ x 20 in.
Roof:	2—	¾ x 13½ x 26½ in.

171

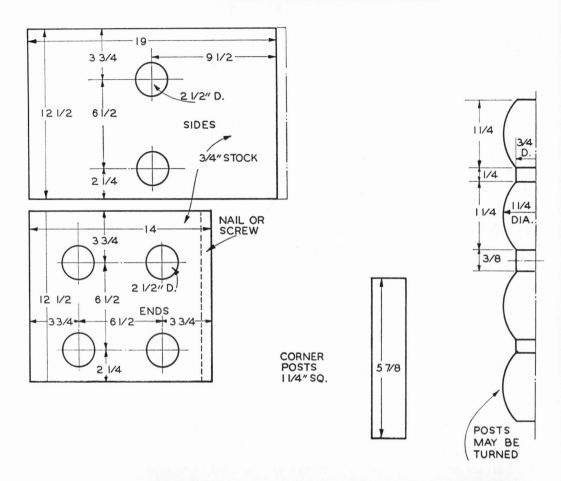

19

3 3/4

9 1/2

2 1/2" D.

12 1/2

6 1/2

SIDES

3/4" STOCK

2 1/4

NAIL OR
SCREW

14

3 3/4

2 1/2" D.

12 1/2

6 1/2

ENDS

3 3/4

6 1/2

3 3/4

2 1/4

CORNER
POSTS
1 1/4" SQ.

5 7/8

1 1/4

3/4 D.

1/4

1 1/4
DIA.

3/8

POSTS
MAY BE
TURNED

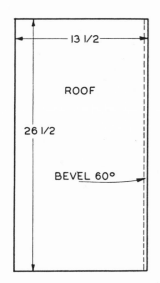

ROOF

13 1/2

26 1/2

BEVEL 60°

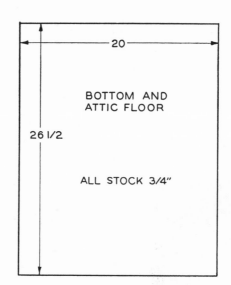

20

BOTTOM AND
ATTIC FLOOR

26 1/2

ALL STOCK 3/4"

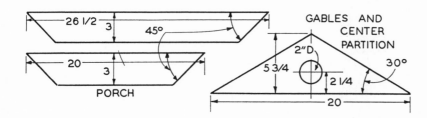

26 1/2   3

45°

20   3

PORCH

GABLES AND
CENTER
PARTITION

2"D.

5 3/4

2 1/4

30°

20

NEST DIVIDERS
EGG-CRATE CONST.
1/2" STOCK

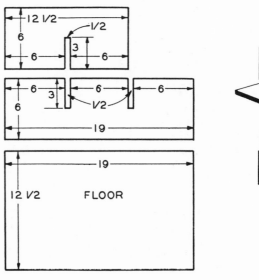

12 1/2   1/2

6

3

6   6

6   3   6   6

6   1/2

6

19

19

12 1/2   FLOOR

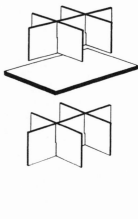

three-story 14-family martin house

This martin house is a familiar sight to all of us and is a
perennial favorite. It is not exceptionally difficult to make
since all of the cuts are straight and only a moderate amount
of accurate fitting is involved. The doors covering the en-

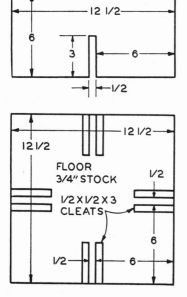

14 – FAMILY
MARTIN HOUSE

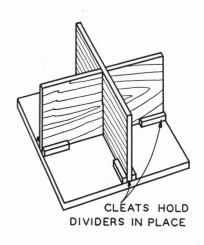

CLOSED

R.H.
SCREW

OPEN

3 1/4 D.

1/4" THICK

DOORS

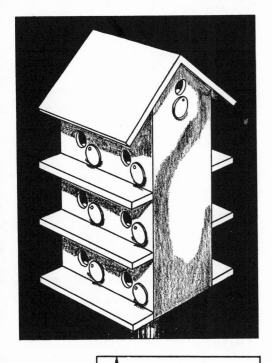

12 1/2

6

3

6

1/2

12 1/2

12 1/2

FLOOR
3/4" STOCK

1/2

1/2 X 1/2 X 3
CLEATS

6

1/2

6

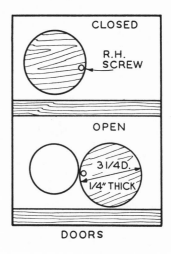

NEST DIVIDERS
EGG-CRATE CONST.
1/2" STOCK

CLEATS HOLD
DIVIDERS IN PLACE

174

trances are an unusual feature. During winter they can be closed to keep out sparrows until the martins arrive. These same doors can be used on the other martin houses.

The entire house, with the exception of the porches, can be made of ¾-inch weatherproof outdoor plywood. Cut the sides and the ends. Nail or screw these together and mount on the ¾-inch base. Nail the porches in place from the inside.

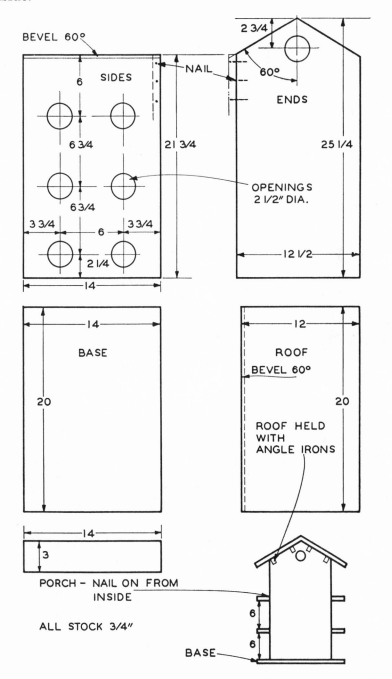

Then make the three inside floors and the three sets of egg-crate nest dividers. Small cleats on the floors will hold the dividers in place as shown. Mount the floors and dividers inside the house. Make the doors and screw them in place. Make the roof last. It is held in place by iron angle brackets and can be easily removed for cleaning in the fall. When the doors are put in the open position, be sure to tighten the screws to keep them from shutting accidently and trapping the birds.

Paint the house white on the outside only; leave the inside natural. Mount it on a pipe or 4 by 4-inch post as explained on page 129. If the house is mounted on a wood post, it can be securely anchored with iron angle brackets. Wood scroll brackets can also be used.

bill of materials

Base:	1—¾ x 14 x 20 in.
Sides:	2—¾ x 14 x 21¾ in.
Ends:	2—¾ x 12½ x 25¼ in.
Porches:	4—¾ x 3 x 14 in.
Floors, inside:	3—¾ x 12½ x 12½ in.
Nest dividers:	6—½ x 6 x 12½ in.
Divider cleats:	24—½ x ½ x 3 in.
Roof:	2—¾ x 12 x 20 in.
Doors:	14—¼ x 3¼-in. dia.

additional housing suggestions

Wrens will build houses in the most unusual places: an old tin can, a shoe, a discarded straw hat. All of these and countless others have been home to a nest full of young wrens. To cater to this whim of the wren, you can attract more of them to your garden perhaps if you make available such houses for them. Here are a few suggestions.

Take a large flower pot, open the hole in the bottom to ¾-inch, drill a small hole near the rim, and hang the pot on a hook screwed into the side of the garage or on a post. Or, take a section of clay drain tile such as farmers use. Plug up both ends with a wood disk, cut a ¾-inch hole in one end, and mount with a wire or steel shipping band on top of a post. You are sure to get a fine family of wrens.

Some people have had good luck with gourds. Select a large gourd, or several if you will. Hollow out the inside through the entrance hole and nail or hang it up most anywhere and you will get tenants.

In some places groups of these gourds are hung together on a dead tree or on special poles and are used by colonies of martins. There are limitless possibilities for improvised houses like this.

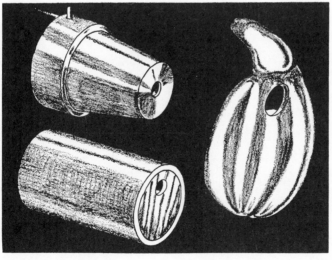

The wren will nest in almost any place. Flower pots, gourds, tiles, and the like make excellent nesting houses.

herring pail wren house

If you are looking for something out of the ordinary in a birdhouse, this wren house should meet with your approval. Although it is not a good policy to use bright colors for serious bird attracting, this birdhouse does lend itself to gay colors. It may become a prized decoration and, strange as it may seem, I put up several decorated in extremely bright colors, just for effect, and had families of wrens in them almost immediately. Of course, the house can be finished in some drab color such as deep brown, and this is perhaps the best thing to do.

Use an ordinary herring pail. Cut a ¾-inch diameter entrance hole. Make the six roof pieces with 65 degree angle sides and toenail them together. Drill a hole through the top for the eye bolt and put on a ball ornament.

Turn the bottom ornamental pieces on a lathe and fasten them with screws from the inside to the bottom of the pail. Drill a hole for the ¼-inch dowel perch and insert the perch. Fasten the hexagonal roof on the top of the pail, driving brass screws in every other section.

If desired, the lower turned ornament can be left off and the house can be mounted on the top of a post or stick.

bill of materials

Pail:	1—7-inch. dia. x 6¾ in. high
Roof:	6— ½ x 5½ x 8¾ in.
Finial:	1—1¾-in. dia. ball
Base:	1— ¾ in. x 7-in. dia.
Base:	1— ¾ in. x 5-in. dia.
Turned part:	1—1¾ in. x 2½-in. dia.

HERRING PAIL
WREN HOUSE

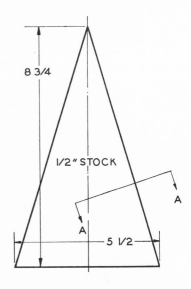

8 3/4

1/2" STOCK

A

A

5 1/2

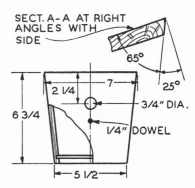

SECT. A-A AT RIGHT
ANGLES WITH
SIDE

65°

25°

2 1/4   7

3/4" DIA.

1/4" DOWEL

6 3/4

5 1/2

1/4 X 5 EYE BOLT

1 3/4 D. BALL

WASHER &
NUT

SCREW

PAIL

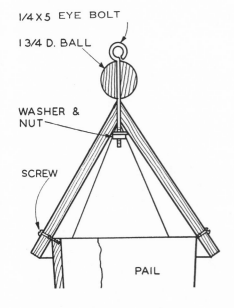

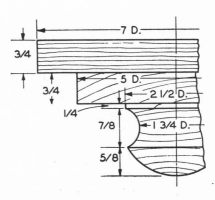

7 D.

3/4

3/4

5 D.

2 1/2 D.

1/4

7/8

1 3/4 D.

5/8

179

Many unique designs and shapes are possible when houses are made of cement and asbestos cement.

Cement houses are not affected by weather and will last indefinitely. They are easy to paint.

ornamental cement birdhouses

The construction of cement birdhouses will offer you a fine opportunity to use your ingenuity. Objects of almost any description can be duplicated such as rustic logs and other items of interesting and intricate shape.

The frame is made either of thin wood slats, as in the smaller house, shown, or of wood parts and wire mesh, as in the log house. In the latter, ½-inch mesh is used but ordinary window-screen wire works better. It can be placed over the larger mesh.

Make a dry mixture of one part cement and three parts asbestos cement, which is used by steam fitters. When thoroughly mixed, add just enough water to make a stiff, putty-like paste. With a putty knife or trowel, spread the mixture on the frames. It will take at least a day for the cement to dry, at which time it will have a white, hard finish that will be weatherproof. The surface can be painted any desired color. For the rustic log, apply the mixture so as to produce a rough surface with deep furrows for the bark. The cement dries slowly so that you can experiment. When dry, apply an undercoat of dark green paint and another coat of dark brown. Rub off the latter to let the green show through and you will have a very natural-looking birdhouse. These houses are cool in summer. Mount them securely because of their weight.

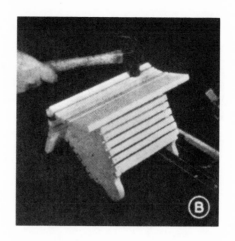

A. A frame made of wood and wire. Cover it with window screening.

B. A house made of wood slats.

C. Mix 1 part cement with 3 parts of asbestos cement.

D. Apply the mixture to the wire frame. Window screen will hold the mixture better than open mesh screen.

E. Moisten wood first, before applying cement to it.

181

birdhouse maintenance in winter

If you let your birdhouses go year after year without attention, they will become dilapidated. They will not only be useless as far as the birds are concerned, but they will be an eyesore in your yard and garden.

A birdhouse should be made so that it is easy to clean. All of the designs in this book are of this type. At the very end of the season, when the birds have definitely left for the south, get a ladder and check each house. Clean it out with a stiff brush and if you have reason to believe that there are lice or other parasites, disinfect it with a strong insect spray. You can cover the holes of a martin house and, if it is on a pole that can be lowered, leave it in the "down" position. It can remain this way until late spring. When the martins are on their way back to your locality, remove the doors and raise the house to the "up" position.

When making your inspection, see how securely the house is mounted. Be sure that the first heavy rain or windstorm will not blow it down. An accident of this kind will not only wreck the house, but it will kill the young or break the eggs. Any house that seems the least bit shaky or loose should be remounted and put up securely.

If the roof of your birdhouse is loose, if the bottom is warped, if a side is cracked, fall is the time to take it down for complete repairs. Renail loose members and replace broken parts if necessary. See that the house is sound throughout. If it needs paint or stain, now is the time to refinish it. When it is dry, return the house to its place outside so that it will have a chance to weather all winter. In this way, when the birds arrive in spring, the newness of the paint and stain will be worn off.

Winter is also a good time to relocate houses and feeders. Tend to the feeders first since they will be in use during the coming winter. You may want to add a few new houses or move some of your old ones. Now is the time to take care of these matters so that everything will be ready when the birds arrive in spring. If you reappraise and improve your program every year, it will be much more effective, because the wants of the birds will be taken care of and you will always be prepared for them.

some helpful hints

winter care of birds

Earlier in this book it was explained how, by feeding birds late into the fall, you can get some of them to spend the winter with you. The importance of food and water to the success of this venture was shown. It was also noted that when the birds have accepted our invitation, we must do more than just feed them; we must also provide shelters for them. Mention was made of the use of cornstalks to provide winter cover.

You can also give them winter protection by making shelter boxes as shown here. These need not be fancy. An old apple

box is suitable. The box is completely closed with an extending shelf-perch at the bottom. The opening is also at the bottom. Before the box is nailed closed, ¼-in dowel perches should be mounted inside. Fill the bottom with straw, excelsior, wood chips, or shavings, and you will have a comfortable, warm retreat for the birds.

Locate the box so that it has a southern exposure and is protected from the north wind. The box can be mounted on the side of the house. Evergreens nearby will be an additional attraction. The roof can extend if you desire, and the entire top can be covered with roofing paper. In addition to this protected box, you might put up a few open shelves in a sunny protected place. The birds will welcome the chance to gather, preen, and hop about here in the warm sun on cold winter days.

brush pile

A favorite pastime of birds is to hunt and scratch around a brush pile. In fall after you have finished pruning, pile the branches as illustrated, with a few sticking out on top to make natural roosts. This makes a fine place for the birds to congregate. If you put a feeder or two near, so much the better. The brush pile can be one of your winter feeding facilities.

A brush pile made in the fall from tree prunings is an excellent bird shelter and hide-away in winter.

John Terres—from the National Audubon Society

the care of sick birds

If a very young bird has fallen out of the nest, handle it as little as possible. Try to get it back into the nest. If this is not possible and if the bird is in immediate danger, place it on a soft cloth in an open box. Keep it warm and away from drafts. If the bird needs food, give it a mixture of one part baby cereal and one part hard-boiled egg every 15 to 20 minutes. Put the food on a smooth stick and place it far back in bird's mouth. Leave the bird where the parent can see it.

If an older bird is sick, there is little that can be done to help it. Return it to cover and nature will take care of it. If it is beyond hope, then it is best to put it out of its misery. To feed older birds, give them a mixture of one part ground raw beef and two parts grated carrots.

The title of this interesting picture could be: "When a fellow needs a friend." Birds should not be handled unnecessarily nor taken out of their nests. If they are blown out of the nest, however, they can be tamed and will stay near your home and yard.

187

Milwaukee Public Museum Photo

natural enemies of wild birds

Just as birds function in the balance of nature to keep down the insect population and the spreading of weeds, so they themselves have natural enemies which prevent them from multiplying in dangerous proportions. An excessive bird population would be just as harmful to man and nature as an oversupply of any other form of plant or animal life.

The animal we think of first as an enemy of the birds is the cat, which does, in fact, kill many of them. It is not possible for you to attract birds and play host to cats simultaneously. One or the other has to go and you will have to make up your mind which it is going to be. If stray cats are prowling about your property, catch them and turn them over to the humane society in your city. It is suggested that you obtain a copy of U. S. Biological Survey Bulletin No. 50, which shows how to make a cat trap.

Although we may think that cats are very destructive of bird life, they do not kill nearly as many birds as starvation, lack of water, and lack of shelter in winter. Man can remove many of these hazards to the birds and by doing so increase their numbers. Disease also kills many birds. For this reason yards, birdhouses, and feeders should be kept clean at all times.

Every city has more than enough sparrows and starlings and there seems to be very little that can be done to get rid of them. They can also be classified as another natural enemy because they compete for the food of the other birds. If trapped, even in large numbers, it seems that there are countless others to take their place. If you would like to trap sparrows, write for   Leaflet No. 61, English Sparrow Control, issued by the United States Department of Agriculture.

Although these birds are pests, remember that they too eat their share of insects and weed seeds and in this way do a lot of good. Possibly it would be best for you to simply decide to put up with them. Since they like to eat on the ground, set aside an area for them away from the regular eating place of the other birds. Keep this place stocked with crumbs and other food. You will be able to bunch the undesirables here, segregating them from the better company. This area may even be on an adjoining vacant lot or some remote corner on your property that is out of sight where they will not disturb the other birds.

wildlife conservation agencies

Here are the leading national agencies that have as part of their goals the protection and study of bird life. You may write to them for further information. In addition, there are any number of local and State Conservation Departments that will be of help to you and with which you can cooperate.

Emergency Conservation Committee
  767 Lexington Avenue, New York, N. Y.

Hawk Mountain Sanctuary Association
  Kempton, Pa.

National Audubon Society
  1130 Fifth Avenue, New York, N. Y.

National Parks Association
  1300 New Hampshire Road N. E.
  Washington D. C.

National Wildlife Association
  1412 16th Street N. W.
  Washington D. C.

Sierra Club
  1050 Mills Tower, San Francisco, Calif.

Wilderness Society
  2144 P Street N. W.
  Washington, D. C.

Useful Reference Books

Guides and Aids to Identification and Location

General

Title	Author
A Field Guide to the Birds	Peterson
A Field Guide to Western Birds	Peterson
A Field Guide to the Birds of Texas	Peterson
A Field Guide to the Birds of Britain and Europe	Peterson
The Pocket Guide to Birds	Cruickshank
Bird's Nests: A Field Guide	Headstrom

Title	Author
Bird's Nests of the West: A Field Guide	Headstrom
Audubon Land Bird Guide	Pough
Audubon Water Bird Guide: Water, Game, and Large Land Birds	Pough
Audubon Western Bird Guide	Pough
A Laboratory and Field Manual of Ornithology	Pettingill
A Guide to Bird Finding West of the Mississippi	Pettingill
A Guide to Bird Finding East of the Mississippi	Pettingill
Naming the Birds at a Glance	Jenks
How to Know the Birds: An Introduction to Bird Recognition	Peterson
A Manual for the Identification of Birds in Minnesota	Roberts
A Field Guide for Locating the Eagle at Cassville, Wisconsin	Ingram
Birds of North America	Robbins

Birds by Region

Title	Author
Birds of America	Pearson
Birds of Columbia	Schauensee
Warblers of North America	Chapman
North American Waterfowl	Day
North American Birds of Prey	Sprunt
A Natural History of East and Central North American Birds	Forbush
Song and Garden Birds of North America	Wetmore
Water, Prey, and Game Birds of North America	Wetmore
Birds East of the Rockies	Reed
Birds of Mexico	Blake
Birds of the West	Booth
Handbook of Eastern North American Birds	Chapman
Audubon Birds of North America	Audubon
Arctic Birds of Canada	Snyder
Birds of Hawaii	Munro
Birds of East and Central America	Williams
Birds of New Zealand	Falla
Birds of the West Indies	Bond
Birds of North America	Brunn and Zim
Ducks, Geese, and Swans of North America	Kortright

Title	Author
American Birds of Prey	Bent
The Shorebirds of North America	Stout
Birds of Colorado	Bailty and Neidrach
Birds of the Blackhills	Pettingill
Eastern Birds	Hausman
Birds of Wisconsin	Gromme
Where to Find Birds in Minnesota	Morrison
Territorial Behavior in the Eastern Robin	Young
The Downy and Hairy Woodpeckers in Wisconsin	Young
Birds of the Northern Forest	Lansdowne
The California Condor	Koford
A Checklist of Iowa Birds	Grant
North American Bird Eggs	Reed
North American Birds	L. and M. Milne

Birds by Name

Title	Author
Flycatchers, Larks, Swallows, and Allies	Bent
Gallinaceous Birds	Bent
Gulls and Terns	Bent
Jays, Crows, and Titmice	Bent
Nuthatches, Wrens, Thrashers, and Allies	Bent
Petrels and Pelicans	Bent
Blackbirds, Orioles, Tanagers, and Allies	Bent
Cuckoos, Goatsuckers, Hummingbirds, and Allies	Bent
Thrushes, Kinglets, and Allies	Bent
Wagtails, Shrikes, Vireos, and Allies	Bent
Woodpeckers	Bent
Wood Warblers	Bent
The Roseate Spoonbill	Allen
The World of the Red-Tailed Hawk	Austing
Life History of the Song Sparrow	Nice
The Herring Gull's World	Tinbergen
The Sandhill Cranes	Walkinshaw
Know Your Ducks and Geese	Shortt and Cartwright
Hawks Aloft	Broun
The Wandering Albatross	Jameson
High Tide and East Wind: The Black Duck	Wright
The Passenger Pigeon	Schorger

The Wild Turkey	Schorger
Puffins	Lockley
Shearwaters	Lockley
The Golden Eagle	Murphy
A Guide to Bird Watching	Hickey

Books for the Study and Enjoyment of Birds

Title	Author
Fundamentals of Ornithology	Van Tyne and Berger
An Introduction to Ornithology	Wallace
Fundamentals of Ecology	Odum
Modern Bird Study	Griscom
Birds	Darling
Bird Biology	MacDonald
Bird Behavior	Goodwin
The Flight of Birds	Storer
A Classification of Birds of the World	Wetmore
A Classification of Recent Birds	Mayr and Amadon
The Book of Bird Life	Allen
Birds and Their Attributes	Allen
Birds Around the World	Amadon
Bird Display and Behavior	Armstrong
A Study of Bird Song	Armstrong
The World of Birds	Fisher and Peterson
Living Birds of the World	Gilliard
The Birds	Heinroth
A Lifetime With the Birds	Greene
An Introduction to Birds	Kieran
Marsh Birds	Bent
Shore Birds	Bent
Wild Fowl	Bent
Diving Birds	Bent
Land Birds	Jaques
Water Birds	Jaques
Water Birds—Bent's life Histories	Collins
Land Birds—Bent's Life Histories	Collins
Birds of the Ocean	Alexander
Waterfowl Tomorrow	Linduska
The Migrations of Birds	Dorst
Migration of Birds	Lincoln
Sea-Birds	Fisher and Lockley
Territory in Bird Life	Howard
Wildlife Conservation	Gabrielson
Population Studies of Birds	Lack
The Life of Birds	Welty
Natural History of Birds	Wing

Birds in Our Lives	Stefferud
The Bird: Its Form and Function	Beebe
Bird Study	Berger
Birds	Gabrielson and Zim
Birds **(Golden Nature Series)**	Vera Webster
Birds	Emlen and Archbald
Biology of Birds	Lanyon
Psychology of Birds	Brutt
Bird Studies at Old Cape May of Coastal New Jersey	Stone
Bird Portraits in Color	Roberts
A Coloured Key to the Wildfowl of the World	Scott
A New Dictionary of Birds of the World	Thomson
Extinct and Vanishing Birds of the World	Greeway

Bird Watching and Documenting

Title	Author
An Introduction to Bird Life for Bird Watchers	Saunders
How to Watch Birds	Barton
A Guide to Bird Watching	Hickey
Bird Watcher's Anthology	Peterson
The Bird Watcher's America	Pettingill
The Bird Watcher's Quiz Book	Collins
Know Your Binoculars	Reichert
Hunting With the Camera	Cruickshank
Manual for Bird Banding	Lincoln
Drawing Birds	Postle
How to Draw Birds	Hunt

Attracting and Caring for Birds

Title	Author
Invitation to Birds	Eifert
Birds in Your Back Yard	Eifert
How to Attract the Birds	Lemmon
The New Handbook of Attracting Birds	McElroy
Your Bird Sanctuary	Peterson
Songbirds in Your Garden	Terres
Looking for a Bird's Nest	Scharff
Attracting Birds from Prairies to Atlantic	Davison
Gardens for Birds	Lemmon
More Birds for Your Garden	Terres

Attracting Birds	McAtee
Landscape Plants That Attract Birds	Ellarsen
Homes for Birds	Kalmbach
Hand—Taming Wild Birds at the Feeder	Martin

Literature and Songs

Title	Author
Thoreau on Birds	Cruickshank
Bird Stories	Cox and Lange
Common Bird Songs (**Manual and Record**)	Borror

Periodicals

Auk	American Ornithology Union
Condor	Cooper Ornithological Society
Wilson Bulletin	Wilson Ornithological Society
Bird Banding	Northeastern Bird-Banding Association
Canadian Field-Naturalist	Ottawa Field-Naturalists' Club
Audubon Field Notes	National Audubon Society
Audubon Magazine	National Audubon Society
British Birds	Witherby, London
Ibis	British Ornithologists' Union

Identification by Song

To help you in identifying birds by their song, as suggested on page 31, you can buy a number of records at your local phonograph shop. They may have a few records on hand for you to examine, or you may find them listed in the shop's record catalogs. Also see above for a book on bird songs.

index

How HIGH To HANG
BIRD HOUSES – Page 12